LET'S EAT
Italian

D1465145

LET'S EAT
Italian

Angelo Capistrani

**Editor:
Wendy Hobson**

foulsham
LONDON • NEW YORK • TORONTO • SYDNEY

foulsham
Yeovil Road, Slough, Berkshire, SL1 4JH

ISBN 0-572-01747-2

Photoset in Great Britain by Typesetting Solutions, Slough, Berks.
Printed in Great Britain by Cox & Wyman Ltd, Reading.

Contents

Introduction

The flavours and aromas of Italian food add sparkle to any kitchen. Making the most of the freshest and tastiest ingredients, there is a variety and enjoyment of food that comes through in every recipe. And because Italian food is so popular, the ingredients are easy to obtain in your local supermarket or delicatessen. Another advantage of Italian cooking for those who are very busy is that many of the dishes can be cooked quickly and easily; no one would think that the delicious results could be obtained with so little work.

The first thing most people think of when they talk about Italian cooking is, of course, pasta, and we have included some wonderful recipes for this favourite of Mediterranean cuisine. If you love pasta, you will love these recipes. If you have tried pasta before and been disappointed, do try it again. There is a whole range of types you can try, of all shapes and sizes, and you are bound to find a favourite. Different shapes take different lengths of time to cook, and often go better with different sauces. Spaghetti or bucatini are perfect with most sauces, for example, spirals and twists catch pockets of smooth creamy sauce. Cooking pasta just right is an art but one that you can soon learn with a little practice. The Italians like pasta cooked *al dente* — 'to the tooth'. This means that it should be just tender but still have a firmness to it. Cooked this way it tastes delicious, and perfectly complements the delicious sauces.

Another favourite Italian export is pizza. A perfect pizza dough is easy to make — great for thrashing out your frustrations on the dough, or quick and easy if you choose to use a food processor. Once you have mastered the basics, you can experiment with your own toppings to incorporate all your favourite things into one meal.

But there is more than this to Italian cooking, as we hope to show you in this book. The pasta dish is usually served as a second course, *I primi,* after the *antipasto* of a colourful and tasty starter to whet the appetite. *I primi* courses may also be a creamy risotto or tasty little gnocchi, tiny dumplings. Next comes the main course, *I secondi,* which is usually a meat, poultry or fish-based course. To refresh the appetite, the Italians then serve a salad course, *insalata,* perhaps a traditional salad or a savoury tart or vegetable dish. Finally comes *I dolci,* the sweet course to round off the meal with a cup of freshly ground coffee.

Ingredients

The ingredients for the recipes in this book will be easy to find at your local supermarket or delicatessen. We have not included any ingredients which are obscure or difficult to locate.

Cannellini Beans

These are available dried or in cans. If you use dried beans, they need to be soaked overnight in cold water, then drained and rinsed. They should then be placed in a saucepan and covered with cold water and boiled for about 40 minutes until tender.

Cheeses

There are many delicious Italian cheeses, some of which are suitable for particular types of cooking.

Bel paese is a cream cheese with a mild flavour, perfect for dips or cooking.

Dolcelatte is a mild and creamy blue cheese.

Mozzarella is a soft, white, rubbery textured cheese which is sold in its own whey to keep it fresh. It is excellent for cooking.

Parmesan is a hard, strongly flavoured cheese which is used in many dishes and frequently sprinkled over finished dishes. You can buy ready grated Parmesan in tubs, but it is best if you grate it freshly yourself.

Pecorino is another hard cheese which is used for cooking and grating. If you find it difficult to buy, you can substitute Parmesan.

Ricotta is a cream cheese used both in savoury and sweet dishes such as cheesecakes.

Herbs and Spices

The Italians use many different herbs and spices in their cooking, most of which are readily available and well known in Britain. Parsley is a great favourite, as well as oregano and marjoram.

If you substitute dried for fresh herbs, halve the quantities, but do not use dried herbs for sprinkling on finished dishes or they will taste dry and unpleasant. It is better to use a different herb or leave them out altogether.

Basil is a favourite in Italian cooking and can be bought there by the bunch. In Britain it is more expensive, although easy to find, so we have limited its use to flavouring. It has a fairly strong flavour so should be used sparingly until you are used to its strength and taste. Dried basil can also be used.

Chillies, both green and dried, are often used. They can be used chopped or whole, in which case they are discarded once the dish is cooked. The seeds are the hottest part and can be used or discarded as you prefer. It is better to discard them at first. Be careful to wash your hands thoroughly after preparing chillies as they contain a strong irritant which will sting if you touch your eyes or mouth after chopping chillies. Also wash the chopping board and knife very thoroughly, or keep a separate one for chopping chillies.

Mushrooms

The Italians often used dried mushrooms, particularly in soups and similar dishes. You can use any dried mushrooms but funghi porcini are favoured. They need to be soaked in hot water for about 30 minutes, then drained before use. They are strongly flavoured and quite expensive so are generally used in small quantities.

Pancetta

Pancetta is an unsmoked cured bacon which is available in delicatessens. You can buy it sliced or in a piece. If you do not have any, you can substitute another cured bacon.

Passata

Passata is simply skinned, seeded and puréed tomatoes. You can make your own from fresh or canned tomatoes by skinning them (see Tomatoes) and rubbing them through a sieve, or you can buy passata in cartons or cans.

Pasta
You can buy pasta fresh or dried, or make your own. There are many types to choose from and some suit particular sauces better than others. It is really a matter of your personal choice and you can substitute your favourites in the recipes if you do not have those specified.

Prosciutto Crudo
This is often better known as Parma ham in Britain, although this is really only one type of prosciutto. It is available in supermarkets and delicatessens.

Rice
Italians most often use rice for risotto dishes, and you should buy Arborio rice, a round-grained Italian rice.

Tomatoes
In Italy, most cooks would use fresh tomatoes as they are freely available, ripe and full of flavour. If you can use fresh tomatoes for any of the recipes, do so. You can skin tomatoes by dropping them into boiling water for a few seconds then into cold water. The skins will quickly peel off. You can deseed them or not, as you prefer.

For most recipes, we have specified canned tomatoes as these plum tomatoes are the sort you would use in Italy. They are already skinned, and are available whole, chopped or sieved (see Passata).

Equipment

No special equipment is needed for Italian dishes; you can use all your usual kitchen equipment.

You will need sharp knives for chopping and preparing fresh ingredients. A garlic press is useful, although not essential, for crushing garlic. Saucepans should be heavy-based, particularly for cooking sauces which have a long slow cooking time. They may burn if cooked in a thin-based pan. A large slotted spoon is required for cooking gnocchi and lifting food from oil or sauces.

Notes on the Recipes

1. Follow one set of measurements only, do not mix metric and Imperial.

2. Eggs are size 2.

3. Wash fresh produce before preparation.

4. Spoon measurements are level.

5. Adjust seasoning and strongly-flavoured ingredients, such as onions and garlic, to suit your own taste.

6. If you substitute dried for fresh herbs, use only half the amount specified.

Appetisers

General Notes

Italian appetisers can be hot or cold, subtle or strongly tasting, but they are always light and chosen to complement the meal to follow.

One of the simplest starters to make is to arrange a selection of Italian meats and vegetables on a platter and serve them with chunks of crusty Italian breads and some olives and Italian pickles. Try salami, mortadella, prosciutto crudo, melon and grilled red peppers.

cappuccino

1 Olives and Anchovies

Ingredients

1 loaf Italian or other crusty bread
100 g/4 oz unsalted butter
100 g/4 oz anchovy fillets, drained
100 g/4 oz black olives, stoned

Method

1. Cut the bread into thick slices and spread with the butter. Lay the anchovies on the top.

2. Serve with the olives.

Serves 4

2 Prosciutto Crudo Rolls

Ingredients

100 g/4 oz Ricotta cheese
6-10 black olives, stoned and chopped
15 ml/1 tbsp chopped fresh basil
Salt and freshly ground black pepper
100 g/4 oz prosciutto crudo

Method

1. Mix together the cheese, olives and basil and season to taste with salt and pepper.

2. Divide the mixture between the slices of prosciutto crudo and roll them up. Serve with crusty bread.

Serves 4

3 | Italian Pickles

Ingredients

6 shallots
2 carrots, thickly sliced
100 g/4 oz small cauliflower florets
1 red pepper, seeded and cut into chunks
½ cucumber, seeded and cut into chunks
450 ml/¾ pt/2 cups white wine vinegar
60 ml/4 tbsp sugar
5 ml/1 tsp mustard seeds
10 black peppercorns
1 dried red chilli pepper, seeded and chopped
Salt

Method

1. Bring a large saucepan of water to the boil and blanch the onions, carrots and cauliflower for 2 minutes. Drain well.

2. Mix together the onions, carrots, cauliflower, pepper and cucumber and place them in screw-top jars with plastic lids.

3. Mix together the remaining ingredients in a saucepan and bring to the boil. Boil for 1 minute then remove from the heat.

4. Pour the hot vinegar over the pickles, leaving a space at the top. Seal the jars and leave to cool completely.

5. Refrigerate for at least 1 week before serving.

6. If you prefer a slightly milder pickle, you can leave the chilli pepper whole and discard it after boiling it with the vinegar and spices.

Makes 1 litre/1 ¾ pts/4 ¼ cups

4 Herby Mushrooms

Ingredients

45 ml/3 tbsp lemon juice
1 clove garlic, crushed
30 ml/2 tbsp chopped fresh parsley
2.5 ml/½ tsp chopped fresh tarragon
120 ml/4 fl oz/½ cup olive oil
Salt and freshly ground black pepper
225 g/8 oz button mushrooms, quartered
½ iceberg lettuce, shredded
½ cucumber, sliced
4 tomatoes, sliced

Method

1. Mix together the lemon juice, garlic, parsley and tarragon. Gradually whisk in the olive oil.

2. Pour the dressing over the mushrooms, cover and marinate in the refrigerator for at least 4 hours, stirring occasionally.

3. Arrange the lettuce, cucumber and tomatoes in a salad bowl. Spoon the mushrooms into the centre and sprinkle with the marinade. Serve the remaining marinade separately.

Serves 4

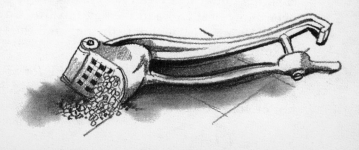

5 Frittata

Ingredients

60 ml/4 tbsp olive oil
3 onions, sliced
400 g/14 oz canned tomatoes, drained and chopped
100 g/4 oz smoked ham, chopped
50 g/2 oz Parmesan cheese, grated
30 ml/2 tbsp chopped fresh parsley
5 ml/1 tsp dried basil
5 ml/1 tsp dried marjoram
Salt and freshly ground black pepper
5 eggs, beaten
30 ml/2 tbsp butter

Method

1. Heat the oil in a heavy-based frying pan over a medium heat and fry the onions for about 10 minutes until golden brown.

2. Add the tomatoes and cook for 5 minutes, stirring continuously. Remove from the pan with a slotted spoon and leave to cool.

3. Mix the ham, cheese, parsley, basil and marjoram into the tomato mixture and season to taste with salt and pepper. Stir in the eggs.

4. Heat the butter in a clean heavy-based frying pan over a low heat and add the egg mixture. Cook for about 10 minutes, without stirring, until the mixture is almost set.

5. Place the frittata under a medium grill for about 1 minute until the top is set but not browned. Serve hot or cold.

Serves 4 to 6

6 Fried Mozzarella

Ingredients

30 ml/2 tbsp olive oil
175 g/6 oz Mozzarella cheese, thickly sliced
30 ml/2 tbsp chopped fresh basil
Juice of ½ lemon
Salt and freshly ground black pepper

Method

1. Heat the oil in a heavy-based frying pan until very hot. Add the mozzarella slices and move them gently so that they do not stick to the pan.

2. As soon as the base is browned, turn over the slices and brown the other side.

3. Place the cheese on a serving plate, sprinkle with basil and lemon juice and season to taste with salt and pepper. Serve immediately.

Serves 4

7 Aubergine Caponata

Ingredients

1 aubergine, cubed
Salt
45 ml/3 tbsp olive oil
1 onion, chopped
1 clove garlic, crushed
1 stick celery, chopped
1 carrot, chopped
1 red pepper, seeded and diced
1 dried red chilli, seeded and chopped
175 g/6 oz passata
15 ml/1 tbsp red wine vinegar
15 ml/1 tbsp sugar
15 ml/1 tbsp capers, chopped
6 olives, stoned and halved

Method

1.   Place the aubergine in a colander and sprinkle generously with salt. Cover with a plate and leave for about 30 minutes so that the bitter juices can drain away. Press out any excess moisture. Rinse and pat dry.

2.   Heat the oil in a heavy-based frying pan and fry the onion, garlic, celery, carrot and pepper for about 5 minutes until soft.

3.   Add the aubergine and fry for a further 5 minutes, stirring occasionally.

4.   Add the chilli and passata and cook, stirring, for a further 3 minutes.

5.   Add the wine vinegar and sugar and cook, stirring, for a further 3 minutes.

6.   Stir in the capers and olives and simmer gently for about 10 minutes until the sauce has thickened. Serve hot or cold.

7.   As a variation, you can also serve this as a vegetable dish.

Serves 4

8 Garlic Toast

Ingredients

8 slices crusty bread
120 ml/4 fl oz/½ cup olive oil
30 ml/2 tbsp chopped fresh basil or parsley
3 cloves garlic, crushed
Salt and freshly ground black pepper

Method

1.   Lay the bread slices in a shallow ovenproof dish.

2.   Mix together the oil, basil or parsley and garlic and season to taste with salt and pepper.

3.   Spoon the flavoured oil slowly over the bread so that it soaks into the slices.

4.   Bake in a preheated oven at 200°C/400°F/gas mark 6 for about 10 minutes until crisp.

Serves 4

9 Crostini

Ingredients

6 slices white bread
45 ml/3 tbsp butter, melted
30 ml/2 tbsp olive oil
15 ml/1 tbsp plain flour
60 ml/4 tbsp milk
50 g/2 oz mushrooms, chopped
50 g/2 oz Parmesan cheese, grated
5 ml/1 tsp anchovy paste
Salt and freshly ground black pepper
6 anchovy fillets
6 olives, stoned and halved
½ red pepper, seeded and cut into strips

Method

1. Cut the bread into 5 cm/2 in rounds with a biscuit cutter. Brush on both sides with melted butter and arrange on greased baking sheets.

2. Bake in a preheated oven at 180°C/350°F/gas mark 4 for about 10 minutes until golden brown, turning once. Remove from the oven and leave to cool on wire racks. Increase the oven temperature to 220°C/425°F/gas mark 7.

3. Heat the oil in a heavy-based frying pan and stir in the flour. Cook, stirring for 1 minute. Whisk in the milk and cook, stirring continuously, for 1 minute until the sauce thickens.

4. Remove from the heat and mix in the mushrooms, half the cheese and the anchovy paste and season to taste with salt and pepper.

5. Arrange the bread circles on a greased baking sheet and top with the mushroom mixture.

Decorate with the anchovies, olives and pepper strips and bake in the hot oven for about 10 minutes until lightly browned. Serve hot.

Serves 4

10 Mussels in Wine

Ingredients

900 g/2 lb mussels, scrubbed and bearded
250 ml/8 fl oz/1 cup dry white wine
30 ml/2 tbsp chopped fresh parsley
50 g/2 oz/¼ cup butter
Salt and freshly ground black pepper

Method

1. Place the mussels in a large heavy-based saucepan with the wine and half the parsley. Cover and heat over a medium heat for about 5 minutes, shaking the pan occasionally, until all the mussels open up. Discard any that do not open.

2. Strain the mussels and reserve the cooking liquor. Remove and discard the empty shells and arrange the mussels in their half-shells on a platter.

3. Meanwhile, bring the cooking liquor to the boil, whisk in the butter and season to taste with salt and pepper. Boil until the liquid reduces slightly then pour it over the mussels. Sprinkle with the remaining parsley and serve with crusty bread.

Serves 4

11 Vegetables in Creamy Anchovy Sauce

Ingredients

50 g/2 oz mushrooms, thickly sliced
1 red pepper, diced
1 stick celery, thickly sliced
50 g/2 oz small cauliflower florets
½ cucumber, cut into chunks
8 spring onions, cut into chunks
600 ml/1 pt/2½ cups double cream
50 g/2 oz butter
2 cloves garlic, crushed
6 anchovy fillets

Method

1. Arrange the vegetables on a serving platter or in individual bowls.

2. Bring the cream to the boil in a heavy-based saucepan then reduce the heat and simmer gently for about 15 minutes until reduced by half.

3. Meanwhile, melt the butter in a small saucepan and fry the garlic for about 3 minutes until soft but not browned. Add the anchovies and cook for about 5 minutes, stirring and mashing with a wooden spoon until the mixture forms a thick paste.

4. Gradually stir the cream into the anchovy mixture, stirring continuously, and simmer over a low heat for about 5 minutes without allowing the mixture to boil.

5. Serve with the vegetables and crusty bread so that the guests can dip their vegetables into the sauce.

Serves 4

12 Aubergine in Tomato and Basil Sauce

Ingredients

1 aubergine, cut into thick sticks
Salt
250 ml/8 fl oz/1 cup olive oil
2 cloves garlic, crushed
400 g/14 oz canned tomatoes, chopped
6 fresh basil leaves, chopped
15 ml/1 tbsp tomato purée
Freshly ground black pepper

Method

1. Place the aubergine in a colander and sprinkle generously with salt. Cover with a plate and leave for about 30 minutes so that the bitter juices can drain away. Press out any excess moisture. Rinse and pat dry.

2. Heat the oil in a heavy-based saucepan and fry the aubergine for about 5 minutes until lightly browned. Remove from the pan and drain on kitchen paper.

3. Add a little more oil to the pan if necessary. Add the garlic and fry gently for 1 minute.

3. Add the tomatoes, most of the basil and the tomato purée and fry for 5 minutes, stirring occasionally. Add a little water to the sauce if it appears too thick.

4. Stir the aubergine back into the sauce and simmer for 5 minutes. Serve sprinkled with pepper and the remaining basil.

Serves 4

Soups

*Italian soups are often a meal in
themselves, made with home-
made stock, lots of fresh
vegetables, and often including
pasta as well. If you have the
time, it pays to make a good stock
to use as the base for your soups,
although you can substitute stock
cubes if necessary. If you make
stock in advance, you can boil it
down to concentrate it so that it
takes up less space, then freeze it
and use it as required, adding a
little extra water with it if
necessary.*

Chicken Stock

Ingredients

1 chicken or chicken carcass
3 carrots
1 onion
3 cloves
2 sticks celery
1 leek, coarsely chopped
5 ml/1 tsp black peppercorns
6 parsley stalks
1 bay leaf

Method

1. Place all the ingredients in a large heavy-based saucepan and just cover with cold water. Bring to the boil, cover and simmer for about 3 hours, skimming if necessary.

2. Strain the stock carefully and return it to the pan. Reserve the chicken meat for other dishes. Boil to reduce the quantity and concentrate the stock, if necessary.

3. Cool quickly, skim off any fat and freeze in suitable quantities or refrigerate and use within 2 days.

4. To make fish or vegetable stock, replace the chicken with some additional vegetables or with fish heads and bones and proceed in the same way.

Makes about 1.75 litres/3 pts/7½ cups

2 Beef Stock

Ingredients

900 g/2 lb beef bones
225 g/8 oz stewing beef
3 carrots
2 onions
3 cloves
2 sticks celery
1 leek, coarsely chopped
2 large tomatoes
5 ml/1 tsp black peppercorns
6 parsley stalks
1 bay leaf

Method

1. Place all the ingredients in a large heavy-based saucepan and just cover with cold water. Bring to the boil, cover and simmer for about 3 hours, skimming if necessary.

2. Strain the stock carefully and return it to the pan. Reserve the meat for other dishes. Boil to reduce the quantity and concentrate the stock, if necessary.

3. Cool quickly, skim off any fat and freeze in suitable quantities or refrigerate and use within 2 days.

Makes about 1.75 litres/3 pts/7½ cups

3 Fennel Soup

Ingredients

45 ml/3 tbsp olive oil
1 onion, sliced
4 fennel bulbs, sliced
45 ml/3 tbsp chopped fresh parsley
1.2 litres/2 pts/5 cups chicken stock
Salt and freshly ground black pepper
50 g/2 oz Parmesan cheese, grated

Method

1. Heat the oil in a heavy-based saucepan and fry the onion for about 5 minutes until soft but not browned. Add the fennel and fry gently for about 5 minutes.

2. Add the parsley and stock and season to taste with salt and pepper. Bring to the boil, cover and simmer gently for about 40 minutes. Serve sprinkled with the cheese.

Serves 4

Chianti Putto

4 Lentil Soup

Ingredients

30 ml/2 tbsp olive oil
75 g/3 oz streaky bacon, chopped
1 onion, chopped
1 carrot, chopped
1 stick celery, chopped
1 clove garlic, crushed
225 g/8 oz/1 cup lentils
1.2 litres/2 pts/5 cups chicken stock
5 ml/1 tsp red wine vinegar
4 tomatoes, skinned, seeded and chopped
1 bay leaf
Salt and freshly ground black pepper
15 ml/1 tbsp chopped fresh parsley

Method

1. Heat the oil in a heavy-based saucepan and fry the bacon, onion, carrot, celery and garlic for about 5 minutes until soft but not browned.

2. Stir in the lentils and add the stock, wine vinegar, tomatoes and bay leaf. Bring to the boil, cover and simmer for about 1 hour, stirring occasionally, until the lentils are tender.

3. Season to taste with salt and pepper, discard the bay leaf and simmer, uncovered, for about 15 minutes until the soup is as thick as you like it. Serve sprinkled with parsley.

Serves 4

5 Pasta and Bean Soup

Ingredients

45 ml/3 tbsp olive oil
1 onion, chopped
1 stick celery, chopped
1 carrot, chopped
1 clove garlic, chopped
100 g/4 oz streaky bacon, chopped
175 g/6 oz dried cannellini beans, soaked overnight
  then drained
1.2 litres/2 pts/5 cups water
5 ml/1 tsp dried thyme
30 ml/2 tbsp chopped fresh parsley
50 g/2 oz pasta shells
Salt and freshly ground black pepper
60 ml/4 tbsp beef stock (optional)
30 ml/2 tbsp Parmesan cheese, grated

Method

1. Heat the oil in a heavy-based saucepan and fry the onion, celery, carrot, garlic and bacon over a low heat for about 10 minutes until very soft but not browned.

2. Add the beans, water, thyme and parsley, bring to the boil, cover and simmer for about 50 minutes until the beans are just tender.

3. Add the pasta and season to taste with salt and pepper. Bring back to the boil and simmer, uncovered, for about 10 minutes until the pasta is cooked, stirring in a little beef stock if necessary to thin the soup. Serve sprinkled with the cheese.

Serves 4 to 6

6 Minestrone

Ingredients

45 ml/3 tbsp olive oil
30 ml/2 tbsp butter
1 onion, chopped
1 clove garlic, crushed
2 carrots, chopped
2 sticks celery, chopped
1 small potato, cubed
50 g/2 oz green beans, cut into 2.5 cm/1 in pieces
1 courgette, cubed
600 ml/1 pt/2 ½ cups chicken or beef stock
400 g/14 oz canned tomatoes, drained and chopped
5 ml/1 tsp chopped fresh basil
2.5 ml/½ tsp dried rosemary
1 bay leaf
Salt and freshly ground black pepper
200 g/7 oz canned cannellini beans, drained
50 g/2 oz Parmesan cheese, grated

Method

1. Heat the oil and butter in a heavy-based saucepan and fry the onion, garlic, carrots and celery for about 5 minutes until soft but not browned.

2. Add the potato, beans and courgette and fry for 3 minutes.

3. Add the stock, tomatoes, basil, rosemary and bay leaf and season to taste with salt and pepper. Bring to the boil, cover and simmer for about 1 hour, stirring occasionally.

4. Add the beans and stir well, adding a little more stock or water if necessary, and simmer, uncovered, over a gentle heat for about 30 minutes. Serve sprinkled with the cheese.

Serves 4

 # Egg and Cheese Soup

Ingredients

1.2 litres/2 pts/5 cups chicken stock
2 eggs, beaten
50 g/2 oz Parmesan cheese, grated
30 ml/2 tbsp chopped fresh parsley
Salt and freshly ground black pepper

Method

1. Bring the stock to the boil in a large heavy-based saucepan.

2. Mix together the eggs, cheese and parsley.

3. Gradually pour the egg mixture into the stock, stirring continuously. Season generously with salt and pepper.

4. Remove the soup from the heat, cover and leave to stand for 3 minutes. Serve with crusty bread.

Serves 4

Vegetable Soup with Meatballs

Ingredients

1.2 litres/2 pts/5 cups vegetable or chicken stock
1 carrot, sliced
1 stick celery, sliced
100 g/4 oz small cauliflower florets
400 g/14 oz canned tomatoes, chopped
15 ml/1 tbsp tomato purée
45 ml/3 tbsp dry red wine
225 g/8 oz minced beef
50 g/2 oz/1 cup fresh breadcrumbs
25 g/1 oz Parmesan cheese, grated
5 ml/1 tsp chopped fresh parsley
2.5 ml/½ tsp dried oregano
Salt and freshly ground black pepper
1 egg, beaten
15 ml/1 tbsp olive oil
100 g/4 oz stelline or small pasta

Method

1. Bring the stock to the boil in a large heavy-based saucepan. Add the carrot, celery, cauliflower, tomatoes, tomato purée and wine, cover and simmer for 10 minutes.

2. Meanwhile, mix together the meat, breadcrumbs, cheese, parsley and oregano and season to taste with salt and pepper. Mix in enough egg to make a firm mixture and press the mixture into small balls the size of walnuts.

3. Heat the oil in a frying pan and fry the meatballs for about 10 minutes until browned all over. Remove from the pan and drain on kitchen paper.

4. Add the meatballs to the soup with the stelline, bring back to the boil and simmer, uncovered, for about 10 minutes until the pasta is cooked.

Serves 4

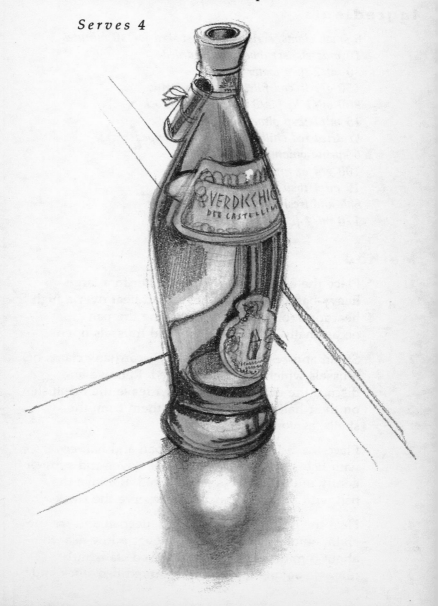

9 | Seafood Soup

Ingredients

6 small clams, scrubbed and soaked for 30 minutes
10 mussels, scrubbed and bearded
30 ml/2 tbsp water
450 g/1 lb cod fillets, cut into strips
900 ml/1 ½ pts/3 ¾ cups fish stock
15 ml/1 tbsp olive oil
½ dried red chilli, seeded and chopped
6 spring onions, sliced
100 g/4 oz mushrooms, sliced
15 ml/1 tbsp cornflour
Salt and freshly ground black pepper
120 ml/4 fl oz/½ cup double cream

Method

1. Place the clams, mussels and water in a large heavy-based saucepan, cover and heat over a high heat for about 5 minutes, shaking the pan occasionally, until the clams and mussels open.

2. Strain and reserve the liquor. Discard any clams or mussels which have not opened. Remove and discard the empty shells. Either leave the shellfish on their half-shells or remove them from the shells, as you prefer.

3. Place the fish strips in a saucepan and half-cover with fish stock. Bring to the boil, cover and simmer gently until the fish is just cooked. Remove the fish with a slotted spoon and reserve the stock.

4. Heat the oil in a heavy-based saucepan and fry the chilli, onions and mushrooms over a low heat for about 5 minutes. Add the reserved clam and mussel cooking liquor, the reserved fish stock and

remaining fish stock and bring to the boil. Simmer for about 5 minutes until reduced slightly.

5. Mix the cornflour with a little of the stock, then stir it into the pan and cook, stirring, until the stock thickens slightly. Season to taste with salt and pepper.

6. Stir in the clams, mussels and fish. Stir in the cream and heat gently until hot, without allowing the soup to boil. Serve immediately.

Serves 4 to 6

10 Fish Soup

Ingredients

45 ml/3 tbsp olive oil
1 onion, chopped
1 carrot, chopped
1 stick celery, chopped
1 clove garlic, crushed
400 g/14 oz canned tomatoes, chopped
15 ml/1 tbsp tomato purée
45 ml/3 tbsp chopped fresh parsley
5 ml/1 tsp dried oregano
1 bay leaf
350 g/12 oz haddock fillets, cubed
2 potatoes, cubed
Salt and freshly ground black pepper
100 g/4 oz shelled prawns

Method

1. Heat the oil in a large heavy-based saucepan and fry the onion, carrot, celery and garlic for about 5 minutes until soft but not browned.

2. Add the tomatoes, tomato purée, half the parsley, oregano and bay leaf and bring to the boil. Simmer gently for 5 minutes.

3. Add the haddock and potatoes and season to taste with salt and pepper. Bring to the boil, cover and simmer gently for about 15 minutes until the fish is cooked.

4. Add the prawns and simmer for a further 5 minutes until the prawns are heated through. Serve sprinkled with the remaining parsley.

Serves 4

Pasta Dishes

General Notes

Pasta — the first thing that springs to most people's minds
when they think of Italian cooking. There are so many
varieties of pasta now available — both fresh and dried —
that you have a wealth of choice when cooking pasta
dishes. Have fun trying them all and choosing your
favourites. And try making your own pasta, too, and see if
you can improve on the flavour.

If you add 15 ml/1 tbsp of olive oil to the water in which
you cook the pasta, it will help stop the pasta sticking
together. Different types of pasta will take different times to
cook, so when you think it is almost ready, keep checking
by biting into a piece or pressing it between your finger
and thumb. Pasta should always be cooked *al dente*, so that
it still has some bite to it and is not soggy and sticky. If you
use fresh pasta, it will only take about 2 minutes to cook.
Dried pasta will take between 6 and 10 minutes.

1 Egg Pasta

Ingredients

400 g/14 oz plain flour
A pinch of salt
4 eggs
10 ml/2 tsp olive oil

Method

1. Make a mound of the flour and salt on a work surface and make a hole in the centre.

2. Break the eggs and pour the oil into the hole and gradually blend in the flour with your fingers until you have a firm dough. Continue to knead until the dough is smooth and elastic.

3. Roll out the dough thickly, then fold it in half and roll it again. Continue to do this until the dough pops when you roll over the fold.

4. Roll out the dough as thinly as possible and cut as you require.

Serves 4

2 Simple Pasta

Ingredients

350 g/12 oz pasta shapes
Salt
90 ml/6 tbsp olive oil
4 cloves garlic, crushed
75 ml/5 tbsp chopped fresh parsley
100 g/4 oz Parmesan cheese, grated
Freshly ground black pepper

Method

1. Bring a saucepan of salted water to the boil, add the pasta, bring back to the boil and simmer for about 10 minutes until the pasta is just tender. Drain well.

2. Meanwhile, heat the oil in a heavy-based pan and fry the garlic over a low heat for about 3 minutes until golden. Remove from the heat and stir in most of the parsley and half the cheese.

3. Toss the pasta into the garlic mixture and stir well to coat it in the oil and herbs. Season to taste with salt and pepper. Sprinkle over the remaining cheese and parsley and serve immediately.

Serves 4

3 Pasta with Cheeses

Ingredients

30 ml/2 tbsp olive oil
1 onion, finely chopped
1 clove garlic, crushed
50 g/2 oz Mozzarella cheese, cubed
50 g/2 oz Parmesan cheese, grated
350 g/12 oz bucatini
Salt and freshly ground black pepper

Method

1. Heat the oil in a heavy-based pan and fry the onion and garlic over a low heat for about 5 minutes until soft.

2. Meanwhile, bring a saucepan of salted water to the boil, add the bucatini, bring back to the boil and simmer for about 7 minutes until just tender.

3. Drain the bucatini and turn into the pan with the onion. Add the cheeses and toss well for about 2 minutes until the cheeses begin to melt. Season to taste with salt and pepper and serve immediately.

Serves 4

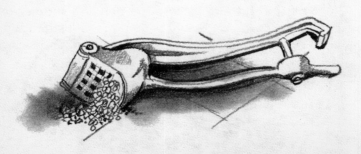

4 | Pasta Salad

Ingredients

450 g/1 lb tomatoes, skinned and chopped
1 onion, finely chopped
2 cloves garlic, chopped
5 green olives, stoned and chopped
15 ml/1 tbsp capers, chopped
60 ml/4 tbsp chopped fresh parsley
30 ml/2 tbsp chopped fresh basil
5 ml/1 tsp dried oregano
1 dried red chilli, seeded and chopped
15 ml/1 tbsp red wine vinegar
120 ml/4 fl oz/½ cup olive oil
Salt and freshly ground black pepper
350 g/12 oz pasta shapes

Method

1. Mix together the tomatoes, onion, garlic, olives, capers, parsley, basil and oregano.

2. Mix the chilli, wine vinegar and olive oil and pour over the vegetables. Toss gently and season to taste with salt and pepper. Cover and refrigerate overnight.

3. Bring a saucepan of salted water to the boil, add the pasta, bring back to the boil and simmer for about 10 minutes until the pasta is just tender. Drain well and toss with the cold tomato sauce.

Serves 4

5 Spaghetti Bolognese

Ingredients

30 ml/2 tbsp olive oil
1 onion, chopped
2 cloves garlic, chopped
1 small carrot, chopped
1 stick celery, chopped
450 g/1 lb minced beef
250 ml/8 fl oz/1 cup dry red wine
400 g/14 oz canned tomatoes, chopped
45 ml/3 tbsp tomato purée
250 ml/8 fl oz/1 cup beef stock
5 ml/1 tsp dried oregano
A pinch of freshly grated nutmeg
Salt and freshly ground black pepper
350 g/12 oz spaghetti
50 g/2 oz Parmesan cheese, grated

Method

1. Heat the oil in a heavy-based saucepan and fry the onion, garlic, carrot and celery over a low heat for about 5 minutes until soft but not browned.

2. Add the beef and fry, stirring, until browned all over.

3. Add the wine and boil for 2 minutes.

4. Add the tomatoes, tomato purée, half the stock and the oregano and season to taste with nutmeg, salt and pepper. Bring to the boil, partially cover and simmer gently for 1 hour until the sauce is thick, adding a little extra stock if necessary.

5. When the sauce is ready, leave it on a low simmer. Bring a large saucepan of salted water to the boil, add the spaghetti, bring back to the boil and

simmer for about 7 minutes until the spaghetti is just tender. Drain well.

6.   Toss the spaghetti with the sauce and serve sprinkled with the cheese.

Serves 4 to 6

Creamy Tagliatelle

Ingredients

350 g/12 oz tagliatelle
Salt
50 g/2 oz butter
150 ml/¼ pt/⅔ cup double cream
2.5 ml/½ tsp freshly grated nutmeg
Freshly ground black pepper
75 g/3 oz Parmesan cheese, grated
45 ml/3 tbsp chopped fresh parsley

Method

1.   Bring a large saucepan of salted water to the boil, add the tagliatelle, bring back to the boil and simmer for about 7 minutes until the tagliatelle is just tender.

2.   Meanwhile, melt the butter with the cream in a heavy-based saucepan over a low heat. Bring to the boil and simmer very gently for 3 minutes. Season to taste with nutmeg, salt and pepper. Stir in the cheese, remove from the heat and stir well until the cheese melts and blends into the sauce.

3.   Drain the tagliatelle well and toss with the sauce. Serve sprinkled with parsley.

Serves 4

7 Spaghetti Carbonara

Ingredients

45 ml/3 tbsp olive oil
1 onion, chopped
1 clove garlic, crushed
4 rashers bacon, chopped
60 ml/4 tbsp dry white wine
350 g/12 oz spaghetti
Salt
4 eggs, beaten
100 g/4 oz Parmesan cheese, grated
15 ml/1 tbsp chopped fresh parsley
Freshly ground black pepper

Method

1. Heat the oil in a heavy-based saucepan and fry the onion for about 5 minutes until soft. Add the garlic and bacon and continue to fry for 5 minutes.

2. Add the wine and boil for 1 minute.

3. Meanwhile, bring a large saucepan of salted water to the boil, add the spaghetti, bring back to the boil and simmer for about 7 minutes until the spaghetti is just tender. Drain well.

4. Add the spaghetti to the onion mixture and stir in the eggs and parsley. The heat from the spaghetti will cook the eggs. Season to taste with salt and pepper and serve immediately.

Serves 4

8 Spaghetti with Garlic and Chillies

Ingredients

350 g/12 oz spaghetti
Salt
30 ml/2 tbsp olive oil
50 g/2 oz butter
1 onion, chopped
2 cloves garlic, crushed
2 dried red chillies, seeded and chopped
1 red pepper, seeded and chopped
Freshly ground black pepper
50 g/2 oz Parmesan cheese, grated

Method

1. Bring a large saucepan of salted water to the boil, add the spaghetti, bring back to the boil and simmer for about 7 minutes until the spaghetti is just tender.

2. Heat the oil and butter in a heavy-based saucepan and fry the onion, garlic, chillies and pepper over a low heat for about 5 minutes until the onion is soft and just beginning to turn golden.

3. Drain the spaghetti well and toss with the sauce. Season to taste with salt and pepper and serve sprinkled with the cheese.

Serves 4

9 | Italian Spaghetti

Ingredients

60 ml/4 tbsp olive oil
2 cloves garlic, crushed
450 g/1 lb tomatoes, skinned, seeded and chopped
½ dried red chilli, seeded and chopped
60 ml/4 tbsp chopped fresh parsley
15 ml/1 tbsp capers, chopped
10 ml/2 tsp chopped fresh basil
5 ml/1 tsp dried oregano
Salt and freshly ground black pepper
10 olives, stoned
5 anchovy fillets, drained and chopped
350 g/12 oz spaghetti

Method

1. Heat the oil in a heavy-based pan and fry the garlic for about 3 minutes until just beginning to brown.

2. Add the tomatoes, chilli, most of the parsley, the capers, basil and oregano and season to taste with salt and pepper. Simmer, stirring, for 1 minute.

3. Add the olives and anchovies and simmer for about 10 minutes, stirring continuously, until the sauce is thick.

4. Meanwhile, bring a saucepan of salted water to the boil, add the spaghetti, bring back to the boil and simmer for about 10 minutes until the spaghetti is just tender. Drain well.

5. Place the spaghetti in a warmed serving dish and pour over the sauce. Toss together and serve sprinkled with the remaining parsley.

Serves 4

10 Spinach Cannelloni

Ingredients

450 g/1 lb cooked spinach, drained
100 g/4 oz Ricotta cheese
Salt and freshly ground black pepper
16 cannelloni tubes
30 ml/2 tbsp butter
30 ml/2 tbsp plain flour
450 ml/¾ pt/2 cups milk
100 g/4 oz Mozzarella cheese, cubed
2.5 ml/½ tsp freshly grated nutmeg
25 g/1 oz/¼ cup dried breadcrumbs
30 ml/2 tbsp chopped fresh parsley

Method

1. Purée the spinach with the Ricotta cheese and season to taste with salt and pepper. Use the mixture to fill the cannelloni tubes and arrange them in a shallow ovenproof dish.

2. Melt the butter in a small heavy-based saucepan and stir in the flour. Cook, stirring, for 1 minute, then gradually stir in the milk and simmer until the sauce thickens. Remove from the heat and stir in the Mozzarella. Season to taste with nutmeg, salt and pepper and pour over the cannelloni.

3. Mix the breadcrumbs and parsley and sprinkle over the cannelloni. Bake in a preheated oven at 200°C/400°F/gas mark 6 for about 30 minutes until heated through and golden brown on top.

Serves 4

11 Spaghetti with Peppers

Ingredients

75 ml/5 tbsp olive oil
1 onion, chopped
1 clove garlic, chopped
1 large red pepper, seeded and diced
1 large green pepper, seeded and diced
750 g/1 ½ lb canned tomatoes, chopped
10 ml/2 tsp chopped fresh basil
½ dried red chilli, seeded and chopped
Salt
350 g/12 oz spaghetti
6 black olives, stoned and chopped
4 anchovy fillets, chopped
15 ml/1 tbsp capers, chopped
30 ml/2 tbsp chopped fresh parsley
Freshly ground black pepper
50 g/2 oz Parmesan cheese, grated

Method

1. Heat the oil in a heavy-based frying pan and fry the onion for 3 minutes until beginning to soften.

2. Add the garlic and peppers and fry for 5 minutes.

3. Add the tomatoes, basil and chilli, bring to the boil, cover and simmer over a low heat for about 20 minutes, stirring occasionally.

4. Meanwhile, bring a large saucepan of salted water to the boil, add the spaghetti, bring back to the boil and simmer for about 7 minutes until the spaghetti is just tender.

5. Add the olives, anchovies, capers and parsley to

the tomato sauce and season to taste with salt and pepper. Stir well and continue to simmer, uncovered, for about 10 minutes.

6. Drain the spaghetti well and toss it with the sauce. Serve sprinkled with cheese.

Serves 4 to 6

12 Penne with Olives

Ingredients

350 g/12 oz penne
45 ml/3 tbsp olive oil
2 cloves garlic, crushed
75 g/3 oz black olives, stoned
15 ml/1 tbsp capers, chopped
15 ml/1 tbsp chopped fresh parsley
2.5 ml/½ tsp freshly ground nutmeg
Salt and freshly ground black pepper

Method

1. Bring a saucepan of salted water to the boil, add the penne, bring back to the boil and simmer until the penne is just tender.

2. Meanwhile, heat the oil in a heavy-based pan and fry the garlic for about 3 minutes until golden.

3. Add the olives, capers and half the parsley and cook, stirring, for 1 minute.

4. Drain the penne and add it to the sauce. Stir together thoroughly and season to taste with nutmeg, salt and pepper. Serve sprinkled with the remaining parsley.

Serves 4

13 Spaghetti with Aubergines

Ingredients

1 large aubergine, diced
Salt
60 ml/4 tbsp olive oil
30 ml/2 tbsp butter
1 onion, chopped
2 cloves garlic, crushed
450 g/1 lb minced beef
400 g/14 oz canned tomatoes
45 ml/3 tbsp tomato purée
5 ml/1 tsp dried oregano
Freshly ground black pepper
350 g/12 oz spaghetti
100 g/4 oz Parmesan cheese, grated
100 g/4 oz Pecorino cheese, grated
50 g/2 oz/½ cup dry breadcrumbs
30 ml/2 tbsp chopped fresh parsley

Method

1. Place the aubergine in a colander and sprinkle generously with salt. Leave to stand for at least 30 minutes to allow the bitter juices to drain away. Rinse in cold water and pat dry.

2. Heat half the oil with half the butter in a heavy-based saucepan and fry the onion and garlic for about 5 minutes until soft and golden.

3. Add the beef and fry for 5 minutes, stirring, until browned all over.

4.	Add the tomatoes, tomato purée and oregano and season to taste with salt and pepper. Bring to the boil, cover and simmer for about 15 minutes, stirring occasionally.

5.	Meanwhile, heat the remaining oil in a heavy-based frying pan and fry the aubergine, in batches if necessary, until lightly browned on all sides. Remove from the pan with a slotted spoon and drain on kitchen paper.

6.	Add the fried aubergine to the tomato sauce and simmer, uncovered for about 10 minutes until tender and well combined.

7.	Bring a large saucepan of salted water to the boil, add the spaghetti, bring back to the boil and simmer for about 7 minutes until the spaghetti is just tender.

8.	Drain the spaghetti well and turn into an ovenproof dish with the sauce. Toss gently together.

9.	Mix together the cheese and breadcrumbs and sprinkle over the spaghetti. Sprinkle with parsley and dot with the remaining butter. Bake in a preheated oven at 190°C/375°F/gas mark 5 for about 10 minutes until crisply browned on top. Serve immediately.

Serves 4

14 Seafood Spaghetti

Ingredients

45 ml/3 tbsp olive oil
2 cloves garlic, crushed
1 onion, finely chopped
120 ml/4 fl oz/½ cup dry white wine
400 g/14 oz canned tomatoes, drained, seeded and chopped
4 oysters, shelled and liquor reserved
25 g/1 oz anchovy fillets, chopped
15 ml/1 tbsp chopped fresh basil
2.5 ml/½ tsp dried oregano
Salt and freshly ground black pepper
350 g/12 oz spaghetti
450 g/1 lb shelled prawns
225 g/8 oz scallops, shelled and halved
15 ml/1 tbsp chopped fresh parsley

Method

1. Heat the oil in a heavy-based pan and fry the garlic and onion for about 5 minutes until soft but not browned.

2. Stir in the wine, bring to the boil and boil for 2 minutes.

3. Add the tomatoes, oyster liquor, anchovies, basil and oregano and season to taste with salt and pepper. Bring to the boil and simmer, uncovered, for about 20 minutes until the sauce is thick, stirring occasionally.

4. Meanwhile, bring a saucepan of salted water to the boil, add the spaghetti and boil for about 10 minutes until the spaghetti is just tender.

5. Stir the oysters, prawns and scallops into the sauce, cover and simmer gently for about 3 minutes until the seafood is cooked through.

6. Drain the spaghetti well then toss it with the sauce and serve sprinkled with parsley.

Serves 4

15 Pasta Spirals with Spicy Sauce

Ingredients

45 ml/3 tbsp olive oil
1 onion, finely chopped
1 small carrot, finely chopped
1 stick celery, finely chopped
1 clove garlic, crushed
100 g/4 oz smoked bacon, chopped
1 dried red chilli, seeded and chopped
225 g/8 oz spinach, steamed and chopped
350 g/12 oz pasta spirals
Salt and freshly ground black pepper
50 g/2 oz Parmesan cheese, grated

Method

1. Heat the oil in a heavy-based pan and fry the onion, carrot, celery, garlic, bacon and chilli over a low heat for about 10 minutes until soft and well combined.

2. Stir in the spinach and continue to cook for a further 4 minutes, stirring frequently.

3. Meanwhile, bring a large saucepan of salted water to the boil, add the pasta, bring back to the boil and simmer for about 10 minutes until the pasta is just tender.

4. Drain the pasta well and toss it with the sauce. Season to taste with salt and pepper and serve sprinkled with cheese.

Serves 4

16 | Mushroom Tortellini

Ingredients

225 g/8 oz/2 cups plain flour
Salt
4 eggs
300 ml/½ pt/1¼ cups milk
5 ml/1 tsp olive oil
100 g/4 oz cooked chicken, minced
50 g/2 oz prosciutto crudo, chopped
50 g/2 oz cooked spinach, chopped
100 g/4 oz Parmesan cheese, grated
75 ml/5 tbsp whipping cream, lightly whipped
Freshly ground black pepper
30 ml/2 tbsp butter
225 g/8 oz mushrooms, sliced
30 ml/2 tbsp chopped fresh parsley

Method

1. Reserve 15 ml/1 tbsp of the flour for the sauce and mix the remainder with a pinch of salt in a pile on a work surface. Make a hole in the centre.

2. Add 3 of the eggs and 15 ml/1 tbsp of milk and the oil and knead until the dough is smooth and elastic. Cover and leave to rest while you prepare the filling.

3. Mix together the chicken, prosciutto, spinach, 30 ml/2 tbsp of cheese and 15 ml/1 tbsp of cream. Season to taste with salt and pepper and mix well.

4. Roll out the dough thinly on a floured surface and cut out 5 cm/2 in circles with a biscuit cutter, covering the dough you are not using with a damp tea towel to prevent it from drying out.

5. Fill the circles with spoonfuls of the chicken filling, damp the edges and seal together into semicircles. Damp the ends and wrap the circles around your finger, sealing the ends together to make little rings. Leave to dry for 30 minutes.

6. Bring a large saucepan of salted water to the boil, add the tortellini, bring back to the boil and simmer for about 4 minutes until the tortellini are just tender.

7. Meanwhile, melt the butter in a heavy-based pan and fry the mushrooms gently for about 3 minutes. Stir in the reserved flour and cook gently, stirring continuously, for 1 minute. Stir in the remaining milk and bring to the boil, stirring, and simmer until the sauce thickens. Stir in the remaining cream and simmer over a very low heat.

8. Drain the tortellini well and place in a warmed serving bowl. Pour over the mushroom sauce and serve sprinkled with the remaining cheese and the parsley.

Serves 4

17 Cannelloni with Tomato Sauce

Ingredients

30 ml/2 tbsp olive oil
1 onion, chopped
1 clove garlic, chopped
1 small carrot, finely chopped
1 stick celery, finely chopped
45 ml/3 tbsp dry white wine
16 cannelloni tubes
Salt
300 ml/½ pt/1¼ cups White Sauce (page 152)
100 g/4 oz cooked chicken, chopped
15 ml/1 tbsp tomato purée
1 egg, beaten
5 ml/1 tsp dried oregano
Freshly ground black pepper
100 g/4 oz Mozzarella cheese, sliced
300 ml/½ pt/1¼ cups Tomato Sauce (page 149)

Method

1. Heat the oil in a heavy-based saucepan and fry the onion, garlic, carrot and celery for about 5 minutes until soft but not browned.

2. Add the wine, bring to the boil and simmer for 2 minutes. Remove from the heat.

3. Meanwhile, bring a large saucepan of salted water to the boil, add the cannelloni, bring back to the boil and simmer for about 7 minutes until just cooked. Drain and rinse in cold water.

4. Mix together the onion mixture with 15 ml/1 tbsp of white sauce, the chicken, tomato purée, egg and oregano and season to taste with salt and pepper.

5. Use the mixture to stuff the cannelloni tubes and lay them in a shallow ovenproof dish. Pour over the remaining white sauce and top with the Mozzarella slices.

6. Bake in a preheated oven at 180°C/350°F/gas mark 4 for about 30 minutes until the cheese is browned and bubbling.

7. Meanwhile, reheat the tomato sauce.

8. Serve the cannelloni immediately with the tomato sauce.

Serves 4

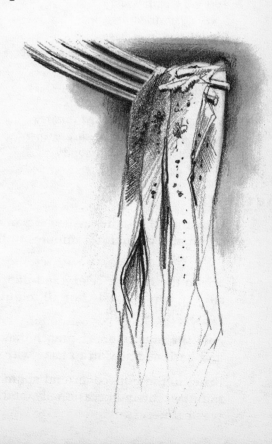

18 Vegetable Lasagne

Ingredients

30 ml/2 tbsp olive oil
1 onion, chopped
1 clove garlic, chopped
100 g/4 oz carrots, chopped
2 sticks celery, chopped
1 red pepper, seeded and diced
100 g/4 oz mushrooms, thickly sliced
100 g/4 oz spinach, chopped
400 g/14 oz passata
5 ml/1 tsp dried oregano
5 ml/1 tsp dried basil
Salt and freshly ground black pepper
30 ml/2 tbsp butter
30 ml/2 tbsp plain flour
300 ml/½ pt/1¼ cups milk
A pinch of freshly grated nutmeg
100 g/4 oz Mozzarella cheese, diced
10 sheets precooked lasagne
50 g/2 oz Parmesan cheese, grated

Method

1. Heat the oil in a heavy-based pan and fry the onion and garlic for 5 minutes until soft but not browned.

2. Stir in the carrots, celery and pepper and cook, stirring continuously, for 10 minutes until the vegetables are soft.

3. Add the mushrooms, spinach, passata, oregano and basil and season to taste with salt and pepper.

4. Bring to the boil, cover and simmer for about 30 minutes, stirring occasionally, and adding a little water if necessary.

5.   Remove the cover and continue to simmer until the sauce has thickened to your liking.

6.   Meanwhile, melt the butter in a small saucepan and stir in the flour. Cook, stirring, for 1 minute. Stir in the milk and bring to the boil then cook, stirring continuously, for about 2 minutes until the sauce is thick. Remove from the heat and stir in the nutmeg and Mozzarella cheese.

7.   Arrange layers of the vegetables, lasagne and sauce in a shallow ovenproof dish, finishing with a layer of cheese sauce. Sprinkle with Parmesan cheese and bake in a preheated oven at 180°C/350°F/gas mark 4 for about 45 minutes until the top is golden brown.

Serves 4 to 6

19 | Chicken Ravioli

Ingredients

45 ml/3 tbsp olive oil
15 ml/1 tbsp butter
3 cloves garlic, crushed
750 g/1½ lb passata
45 ml/3 tbsp tomato purée
5 ml/1 tsp dried basil
5 ml/1 tsp dried rosemary
Salt and freshly ground black pepper
100 g/4 oz minced beef
100 g/4 oz cooked chicken, chopped
50 g/2 oz cooked ham, chopped
50 g/2 oz salami, chopped
30 ml/2 tbsp chopped fresh parsley
3 eggs
450 g/1 lb plain flour
250 ml/8 fl oz/1 cup water

Method

1. Heat 30 ml/2 tbsp oil with the butter in a heavy-based saucepan and fry 2 cloves of garlic for 1 minute.

2. Add the passata, tomato purée, basil and rosemary and season to taste with salt and pepper. Bring to the boil, cover and simmer for 30 minutes, stirring occasionally.

3. Remove the cover and continue to simmer until the sauce has thickened to the consistency you prefer.

4. Meanwhile, brown the beef with the remaining garlic in a heavy-based frying pan. Remove from the heat and mix in the chicken, ham, salami, parsley and 1 egg. Cool and refrigerate until required.

5. Place the flour and a pinch of salt on a work surface and make a well in the centre. Add the remaining eggs and half the water and knead to a firm dough, adding as much of the remaining water as necessary. Knead well, roll out and fold in half then roll again until the pasta is elastic and smooth.

6. Divide the pasta in half and roll out into two large squares. Place spoonfuls of the filling at regular intervals over the surface of one square and brush between the filling with water. Place the second square over the top and press down between the filling to seal the two sheets. Cut out into squares with a fluted pastry cutter or knife.

7. Bring a large saucepan of salted water to the boil, add the ravioli, in batches if necessary, and cook for about 4 minutes. Remove and drain well.

8. Add the ravioli to the sauce and simmer gently for about 10 minutes. Serve immediately.

Serves 6

Seafood

There is a range of dishes in Italian cuisine for both sea and freshwater fish and many types of seafood. Prawns and squid are favourites, and you can cook almost any firm-fleshed fish with a delicious Italian sauce.

1 Mussels in Wine

Ingredients

48 mussels, scrubbed and bearded
1 clove garlic, crushed
15 ml/1 tbsp olive oil
250 ml/8 fl oz/1 cup dry white wine
30 ml/2 tbsp chopped fresh parsley

Method

1. Place the mussels, garlic, oil and wine in a large saucepan, cover and heat over a medium heat for about 5 minutes, shaking the pan occasionally, until the mussels open. Discard any that remain closed.

2. Remove the top shell from the mussels and arrange them in their bottom shells on a serving plate.

3. Meanwhile, bring the liquor in the pan to the boil and boil until reduced to about 60 ml/4 tbsp. Spoon over the mussels and serve sprinkled with parsley.

Serves 4

2 Fried Squid Rings

Ingredients

450 g/1 lb squid
1 egg, beaten
15 ml/1 tbsp milk
100 g/4 oz/1 cup dry breadcrumbs
Olive oil for deep-frying
1 lemon, sliced
1 quantity Tartare Sauce (page 156)

Method

1. To prepare squid, pull the head and contents of the body away from the body. Cut off and reserve the tentacles. Discard the head and body contents and the clear piece of cartilage. Remove and discard the outer skin.

2. Cut the squid into rings. Wash and pat dry.

3. Beat the egg and milk together. Add the squid and coat well.

4. Dip the squid rings in the breadcrumbs and leave to stand for about 10 minutes while you heat the oil.

5. Heat the oil in a deep heavy-based pan. Make sure you do not fill the pan too full as the squid rings will spit when cooked. Add the squid rings a few at a time and fry for about 1 minute until golden brown. Remove from the pan and drain on kitchen paper.

6. Garnish with lemon slices and serve hot with tartare sauce.

Serves 4

3 | Marinated Squid

Ingredients

450 g/1 lb squid, clean and cut into rings (see page 64)
90 ml/6 tbsp olive oil
Juice of 1 large lemon
5 ml/1 tsp white wine vinegar
1 clove garlic, crushed
30 ml/2 tbsp chopped fresh parsley
15 ml/1 tbsp chopped fresh basil
Salt and freshly ground black pepper

Method

1. Bring a saucepan of water to the boil, add the squid rings and simmer for about 20 minutes until the squid is tender. Drain well and pat dry.

2. Mix together the remaining ingredients and season to taste with salt and pepper. Add the squid rings and stir thoroughly. Cover and refrigerate for 24 hours, stirring occasionally.

Serves 4

Prawns and Seafood in Batter

Ingredients

225 g/8 oz/1 cup plain flour
2.5 ml/½ tsp salt
A pinch of freshly ground black pepper
A pinch of cayenne pepper
250 ml/8 fl oz/1 cup warm water
15 ml/1 tbsp olive oil
2 egg whites
375 g/12 oz squid, cleaned and cut into rings (see page 64)
225 g/8 oz shelled prawns
225 g/8 oz haddock fillets, diced
Olive or sunflower oil for deep-frying
1 lemon, sliced
1 quantity Tartare Sauce (page 156)

Method

1. Mix together the flour and salt and season with pepper and cayenne. Mix in the water and oil and whisk to a smooth batter. Cover and leave to stand for 1 hour.

2. Whisk the egg whites until stiff and fold them into the batter.

3. Dip the seafood into the batter a few pieces at a time and fry in the hot oil for about 2 minutes until golden brown. Drain well on kitchen paper, garnish with lemon slices and serve hot with tartare sauce.

Serves 4

5 Crispy Sardines

Ingredients

100 g/4 oz/½ cup butter
2.5 ml/½ tsp lemon juice
15 ml/1 tbsp chopped fresh parsley
1 clove garlic, finely chopped
Salt and freshly ground black pepper
75 g/3 oz/¾ cup plain flour
2 eggs, beaten
45 ml/3 tbsp milk
24 sardines, boned
100 g/4 oz/1 cup dried breadcrumbs
45 ml/3 tbsp olive oil
1 lemon, sliced

Method

1. Mix together the butter, lemon juice, parsley and garlic and season to taste with salt and pepper. Blend together well and use a piece of greaseproof paper to roll the flavoured butter into a thick sausage shape. Chill while you prepare the fish.

2. Season the flour with salt and pepper. Beat the eggs and milk together.

3. Dip the sardines in the flour and shake off the excess. then dip them in the egg mixture, then the breadcrumbs.

4. Heat the oil and fry the sardines for about 5 minutes until cooked through and brown and crispy.

5. Arrange the sardines on a warmed serving platter and top with slices of the herb butter. Serve garnished with lemon slices.

Serves 4

6 Marinated Haddock

Ingredients

75 ml/5 tbsp olive oil
30 ml/2 tbsp lemon juice
1 onion, finely chopped
6 black peppercorns
Salt
450 g/1 lb haddock fillets
45 ml/3 tbsp plain flour
Freshly ground black pepper
2 eggs, beaten
30 ml/2 tbsp milk
100 g/4 oz/1 cup dried breadcrumbs
75 g/3 oz butter
30 ml/2 tbsp chopped fresh parsley
1 lemon, cut into wedges

Method

1. Mix together the oil, lemon juice, onion and peppercorns and season with salt to make a marinade. Add the haddock, cover and marinate for at least 1 hour.

2. Remove the haddock from the marinade and drain thoroughly.

3. Season the flour with salt and pepper. Beat together the eggs and milk.

4. Dip the fillets in flour, then egg, then breadcrumbs.

5. Heat the butter with the strained oil from the marinade in a heavy-based pan and fry the haddock for about 8 minutes until cooked through and crispy. Transfer the haddock to a warmed serving dish.

6. Add the parsley to the pan and stir over a medium heat until the butter begins to brown. Pour over the fish and serve garnished with lemon wedges.

Serves 4

 Trout with Lemon and Rosemary

Ingredients

1 large trout
1 lemon, sliced
1 large sprig rosemary
Salt and freshly ground black pepper
1 clove garlic, finely chopped
250 ml/8 fl oz/1 cup dry white wine
15 ml/1 tbsp chopped fresh parsley

Method

1. Place the lemon slices and rosemary in the cavity of the fish. Season it well with salt and pepper and lay it in a shallow ovenproof dish.

2. Sprinkle the fish with the garlic and pour over the wine. Cover and bake in a preheated oven at 180°C/350°F/gas mark 4 for about 35 minutes until cooked through and tender. Serve immediately.

Serves 4

8 Cod with Courgettes

Ingredients

45 ml/3 tbsp olive oil
3 courgettes, sliced
1 onion, chopped
1 clove garlic, crushed
1 carrot, chopped
1 stick celery, chopped
400 g/14 oz passata
15 ml/1 tbsp chopped fresh basil
15 ml/1 tbsp chopped fresh parsley
450 g/1 lb cod fillets, cut into chunks
Salt and freshly ground black pepper
45 ml/3 tbsp dried breadcrumbs
25 g/1 oz/2 tbsp butter

Method

1. Heat the oil in a flameproof dish and fry the courgettes for about 2 minutes until lightly browned. Remove from the pan and drain on kitchen paper.

2. Add the onion, garlic, carrot and celery to the pan and cook over a low heat for about 10 minutes until soft but not browned.

3. Add the passata, basil and parsley, bring to the boil, cover and simmer gently for 5 minutes.

4. Add the courgettes and fish and season to taste with salt and pepper. Cover and simmer for about 30 minutes until the fish is cooked, adding a little water to the sauce if necessary.

5. Sprinkle with the breadcrumbs and dot with butter. Heat under a hot grill for a few minutes until the top begins to brown. Serve immediately.

Serves 4

Poultry

Chicken, duck and many other poultry meats are popular in Italy, often served with rich sauces of tomatoes and olives. Any of the recipes will taste delicious cooked with chicken.

Chicken with Wine and Olives

Ingredients

30 ml/2 tbsp olive oil
1 onion, chopped
1 clove garlic, chopped
1 carrot, finely chopped
1 stick celery, finely chopped
4 chicken breasts, skinned and boned
120 ml/4 fl oz/½ cup dry white wine
120 ml/4 fl oz/½ cup chicken stock
10 green olives, stoned
10 black olives, stoned
30 ml/2 tbsp chopped fresh parsley

Method

1. Heat the oil in a heavy-based pan and fry the onion, garlic, carrot and celery over a low heat for about 10 minutes until soft. Add the chicken breasts and cook over a medium heat until browned all over.

2. Add the wine, bring to the boil and simmer for 2 minutes.

3. Add the chicken stock, bring back to the boil, cover and simmer gently for about 20 minutes until the chicken is cooked through and tender.

4. Add the olives and half the parsley and simmer, uncovered, for a further 10 minutes. Serve garnished with the remaining parsley.

Serves 4

Chicken in Marsala Cream

Ingredients

15 ml/1 tbsp olive oil
15 ml/1 tbsp butter
4 chicken breasts, skinned and boned
Salt and freshly ground black pepper
100 g/4 oz Mozzarella cheese, sliced
12 capers
4 anchovy fillets, drained
30 ml/2 tbsp chopped fresh parsley
1 clove garlic, crushed
60 ml/4 tbsp marsala
150 ml/¼ pt/⅔ cup cream

Method

1. Heat the oil and butter in a heavy-based pan. Season the chicken breasts with salt and pepper and fry them for about 15 minutes until browned on both sides and cooked through.

2. Arrange the cheese on top of the chicken and top with the capers and anchovies. Sprinkle with parsley, cover and cook over a low heat for about 5 minutes until the cheese is just beginning to melt. Transfer the chicken to a warmed serving platter and keep warm.

3. Add the garlic to the pan and fry for 1 minute. Stir in the marsala, bring to the boil and simmer for 1 minute. Stir in the cream and heat gently, stirring continuously, for about 5 minutes. Season to taste with salt and pepper. Spoon the sauce over the chicken and serve immediately.

Serves 4

3 Chicken Cacciatore

Ingredients

30 ml/2 tbsp olive oil
15 ml/1 tbsp butter
1 chicken, cut into 8 portions
1 onion, chopped
1 clove garlic, crushed
100 g/4 oz mushrooms, sliced
120 ml/4 fl oz/½ cup dry white wine
15 ml/1 tbsp white wine vinegar
150 ml/¼ pt/⅔ cup chicken stock
400 g/14 oz passata
30 ml/2 tbsp chopped fresh basil
Salt and freshly ground black pepper
10 black olives, stoned
30 ml/2 tbsp chopped fresh parsley

Method

1. Heat the oil and butter in a heavy-based pan and fry the chicken pieces until browned on all sides. Transfer to a flameproof casserole.

2. Add the onion and garlic to the pan and fry for 5 minutes until soft. Add the mushrooms and fry for 2 minutes. Add the wine and wine vinegar and simmer for 5 minutes.

3. Add the chicken stock, passata and basil and season to taste with salt and pepper. Bring to the boil and simmer for 5 minutes.

4. Pour the tomato sauce over the chicken, cover and simmer gently for about 40 minutes until the chicken is tender.

5. Remove the lid and continue to boil for about 5 minutes until the sauce has thickened. Add the

olives and parsley and simmer for a further 2 minutes before serving.

Serves 4

Crispy Fried Duck

Ingredients

4 duck breasts
Salt and freshly ground black pepper
30 ml/2 tbsp olive oil
3 cloves garlic, crushed
100 g/4 oz/1 cup dried breadcrumbs
50 g/2 oz Parmesan cheese, grated
50 g/2 oz/¼ cup butter

Method

1. Season the duck breasts generously with salt and pepper.

2. Heat the oil in a heavy-based pan and add the garlic and duck breasts. Fry over a medium heat until the duck is browned all over, then reduce the heat, cover and fry for about 25 minutes until the duck is cooked through and tender, basting occasionally with the oil.

3. Transfer the duck to a shallow flameproof serving dish and sprinkle with the breadcrumbs and cheese. Dot with the butter and place under a hot grill for about 5 minutes until the topping is crispy and lightly browned.

Serves 4

5 Pheasant with Chestnuts and Oranges

Ingredients

2 oven-ready pheasants
Salt and freshly ground black pepper
100 g/4 oz/½ cup butter
30 ml/2 tbsp olive oil
1 onion, finely chopped
1 clove garlic, crushed
Grated rind and juice of 1 orange
30 ml/2 tbsp plain flour
150 ml/¼ pt/⅔ cup chicken stock
90 ml/6 tbsp marsala
90 ml/6 tbsp dry white wine
100 g/4 oz cooked chestnuts
2 oranges, peeled and cut into segments

Method

1.   Season the pheasants with salt and pepper.

2.   Heat the butter and oil and fry the onion and garlic for 3 minutes until just soft. Add the pheasants to the pan and brown them all over then transfer them to a flameproof roasting tin.

3.   Add the orange rind and juice to the pan and heat through gently then pour it over the pheasants. Bake them in a preheated oven at 190°C/375°F/ gas mark 5 for about 1 ½ hours until tender, basting occasionally.

4. Place the pheasants on a warmed serving plate and keep them warm.

5. Skim the fat from the roasting tin and stir in the flour over a low heat. Cook, stirring, for 1 minute.

6. Add the stock, marsala and wine and bring to the boil, stirring. Simmer gently for 5 minutes, stirring frequently. Add the chestnuts and oranges and simmer over a very low heat for 10 minutes, stirring occasionally. Spoon the chestnuts and oranges around the pheasants, pour over the remaining sauce and serve immediately.

Serves 4

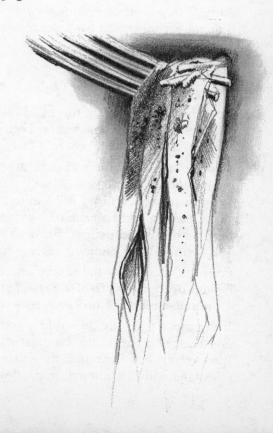

6 | Turkey Casserole

Ingredients

30 ml/2 tbsp olive oil
4 turkey fillets
2 onions, sliced
2 cloves garlic, crushed
225 g/8 oz pancetta, cubed
1 fennel bulb, sliced
225 g/8 oz mushrooms, sliced
175 ml/6 fl oz/¾ cup chicken stock
45 ml/3 tbsp passata
30 ml/2 tbsp chopped fresh parsley
Salt and freshly ground black pepper
15 ml/1 tbsp butter
15 ml/1 tbsp plain flour

Method

1. Heat the oil and fry the turkey fillets for a few minutes until well browned on both sides. Transfer them to a flameproof casserole dish.

2. Add the onions, garlic and pancetta to the pan and fry for about 5 minutes until soft. Add the fennel and mushrooms and fry for 3 minutes. Add the stock, passata and half the parsley and season to taste with salt and pepper. Bring to the boil, cover and simmer for 5 minutes, stirring well.

3. Pour the sauce over the turkey and cook in a pre-heated oven at 180°C/350°F/gas mark 4 for about 45 minutes until the turkey is cooked through.

4. If the sauce is a little thin, mix together the butter and flour and stir it into the casserole, a little at a time, over a low heat until the sauce thickens. Serve sprinkled with the remaining parsley.

Serves 4 to 6

Meat

Veal is particularly popular in Italian cuisine and you can make some delicious and quick dishes with veal escalope, or you can substitute turkey fillets, which are widely available in supermarkets, although these will take slightly longer to cook.

1 Osso Bucco

Ingredients

45 ml/3 tbsp olive oil
1 onion, chopped
1 clove garlic, crushed
1 stick celery, chopped
1 carrot, chopped
4 pieces shin of beef
15 ml/1 tbsp plain flour
30 ml/2 tbsp butter
250 ml/8 fl oz/1 cup dry white wine
400 g/14 oz passata
15 ml/1 tbsp tomato purée
250 ml/8 fl oz/1 cup beef stock
15 ml/1 tbsp chopped fresh basil
5 ml/1 tsp dried rosemary
1 bay leaf
Salt and freshly ground black pepper
30 ml/2 tbsp chopped fresh parsley
5 ml/1 tsp lemon juice

Method

1. Heat the oil in a heavy-based pan and fry the onion, garlic, celery and carrot for about 5 minutes until soft. Transfer to a flameproof casserole dish.

2. Toss the beef in the flour. Add the butter to the pan and when it is hot, add the beef and fry until it is browned on all sides. Transfer to the casserole dish.

3. Add the wine to the pan and boil for 1 minute. Add the passata, tomato purée, stock, basil, rosemary and bay leaf and season to taste with salt and pepper. Bring to the boil and simmer for 2 minutes, then pour over the beef. Cover and cook in a preheated oven at 180°C/350°F/gas mark 4 for about 2 hours until the beef is very tender.

4. Transfer the beef to a warmed serving dish. Stir half the parsley and the lemon juice into the casserole dish and simmer, uncovered, until the sauce has thickened to your liking. Spoon over the beef and serve sprinkled with the remaining parsley.

Serves 4

2 Veal with Tomato and Parmesan

Ingredients

90 ml/6 tbsp olive oil
1 onion, chopped
2 cloves garlic, crushed
1 green pepper, seeded and chopped
1 stick celery, chopped
1 carrot, chopped
400 g/14 oz canned tomatoes, chopped
15 ml/1 tbsp tomato purée
15 ml/1 tbsp chopped fresh parsley
5 ml/1 tsp chopped fresh basil
Salt and freshly ground black pepper
4 veal escalopes
15 ml/1 tbsp plain flour
1 egg, beaten
50 g/2 oz/½ cup dried breadcrumbs
50 g/2 oz Parmesan cheese, grated

Method

1. Heat half the oil in a heavy-based pan and fry the onion, garlic, pepper, celery and carrot for 5 minutes until soft.

2. Add the tomatoes, tomato purée, parsley and basil and season to taste with salt and pepper. Bring to the boil, cover and simmer, stirring occasionally, for about 45 minutes until the sauce is thick.

3. Dust the escalopes with flour, dip in the egg and coat in breadcrumbs. Heat the remaining oil and fry the escalopes for about 5 minutes until cooked and crispy.

4. Spoon the tomato sauce into a serving dish and top with the escalopes. Serve sprinkled with Parmesan cheese.

Serves 4

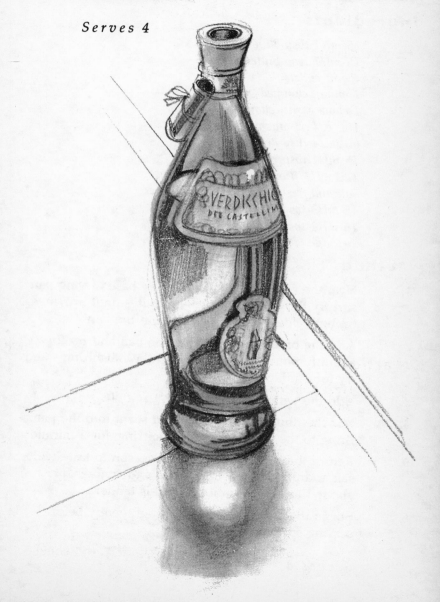

3 | Veal Scallopine

Ingredients

15 ml/1 tbsp olive oil
15 ml/1 tbsp butter
4 veal cutlets
1 onion, chopped
1 clove garlic, chopped
100 g/4 oz mushrooms, sliced
60 ml/4 tbsp dry white wine
15 ml/1 tbsp plain flour
120 ml/4 fl oz/½ cup chicken stock
Salt and freshly ground black pepper
45 ml/3 tbsp double cream
15 ml/1 tbsp chopped fresh parsley

Method

1. Heat the oil and butter in a heavy-based frying pan and fry the cutlets for a few minutes until browned on both sides. Remove them from the pan.

2. Add the onions and garlic to the pan and fry for about 5 minutes until soft. Add the mushrooms and fry for 1 minute.

3. Add the wine and simmer for 1 minute.

4. Mix the flour into the stock and stir it into the pan. Bring to the boil and simmer, stirring, for 2 minutes.

5. Return the veal to the pan and season to taste with salt and pepper. Cover the pan and simmer for about 10 minutes until the veal is tender.

6. Stir in the cream and heat through gently before serving sprinkled with parsley.

Serves 4

4 # Veal with Spinach and Mozzarella

Ingredients

100 g/4 oz butter
2 cloves garlic, crushed
75 ml/5 tbsp dry white wine
400 g/14 oz passata
Salt and freshly ground black pepper
100 g/4 oz spinach, shredded
60 ml/4 tbsp plain flour
4 veal cutlets
15 ml/1 tbsp olive oil
100 g/4 oz Mozzarella cheese, sliced

Method

1. Heat half the butter in a heavy-based pan and fry the garlic for 1 minute. Add the wine, bring to the boil and simmer for 1 minute. Stir in the passata and season to taste with salt and pepper. Bring to the boil and simmer, uncovered, for about 10 minutes.

2. Meanwhile, rinse the spinach in water and shake dry. Place in a heavy-based saucepan and steam for 5 minutes. Stir in the remaining butter.

3. Heat the oil in a heavy-based pan and fry the veal cutlets for about 8 minutes until golden brown on both sides.

4. Transfer the veal to the tomato sauce, placing them carefully on top of the sauce. Spoon the spinach over the veal and top with the cheese slices. Cover and simmer over a very low heat for about 10 minutes. Serve immediately.

Serves 4

Cold Veal with Tuna Sauce

Ingredients

1.5 kg/3 lb veal joint, boned and rolled
2 cloves garlic, sliced
1 onion, quartered
1 stick celery, quartered
1 carrot, quartered
250 ml/8 fl oz/1 cup dry white wine
1 egg
1 egg yolk
30 ml/2 tbsp lemon juice
30 ml/2 tbsp white wine vinegar
250 ml/8 fl oz/1 cup vegetable oil
Salt and freshly ground black pepper
15 ml/1 tbsp chopped capers
25 g/1 oz anchovies, drained and chopped
200 g/7 oz canned tuna, drained and flaked
15 ml/1 tbsp chopped fresh parsley
6 black olives, stoned and chopped

Method

1. Make cuts in the veal and press in the slices of garlic.

2. Place the veal in a large heavy-based saucepan with the onion, celery, carrot and wine and just cover the meat with water. Bring to the boil, cover and simmer gently for about 1½ hours until the veal is tender.

3. Leave the veal to cool in the stock then refrigerate in the stock overnight. Remove and drain veal and slice it thinly.

4.   Place the egg, egg yolk, lemon juice and wine vinegar in a blender and process until well blended. With the motor running, gradually add the oil in a steady stream to make the mayonnaise.

5.   Mix together the capers, anchovies, tuna, parsley and olives and fold it into the mayonnaise.

6.   Spoon one-third of the tuna mayonnaise into a serving dish and top with half the veal slices. Cover with a further one-third of the tuna mayonnaise and top with the remaining veal. Finish with the remaining tuna mayonnaise. Refrigerate for at least 3 hours before serving.

Serves 4

6   Creamy Pork in Wine

Ingredients

30 ml/2 tbsp olive oil
2 onions, sliced
1 clove garlic, crushed
450 g/1 lb pork loin, cubed
15 ml/1 tbsp plain flour
250 ml/8 fl oz/1 cup dry white wine
Salt and freshly ground black pepper
60 ml/4 tbsp double cream
15 ml/1 tbsp butter (optional)

Method

1. Heat the oil in a heavy-based pan and fry the onions and garlic for about 5 minutes until soft.

2. Dust the pork in the flour, add to the pan and fry for about 4 minutes until browned on all sides.

3. Add the wine and bring to the boil, stirring well. Season to taste with salt and pepper. Cover and simmer for about 30 minutes until the pork is tender.

4. Stir in the cream and heat through gently, stirring well. If the sauce needs thickening, mix together the butter with the remaining flour, stir it into the sauce and cook for 3 minutes. Serve immediately.

Serves 4

7 Liver with Onions

Ingredients

45 ml/3 tbsp olive oil
15 ml/1 tbsp butter
4 onions, sliced
60 ml/4 tbsp plain flour
Salt and freshly ground black pepper
450 g/1 lb calves' liver, sliced
30 ml/2 tbsp chopped fresh parsley

Method

1. Heat 30 ml/2 tbsp of oil with the butter in a heavy-based pan and fry the onions for about 15 minutes until lightly browned.

2. Meanwhile, season the flour with salt and pepper and toss the liver in the flour until lightly dusted. Shake off any excess. Heat the remaining oil in a second pan and fry the liver slices over a high heat for a few minutes until lightly browned on all sides.

3. Transfer the liver to the pan with the onions and fry, stirring gently, for about 4 minutes until the liver is just cooked through but still tender. Season to taste with salt and pepper and serve sprinkled with parsley.

Serves 4

Vegetable Dishes

Many vegetable dishes can double as tasty appetisers to start off a meal. When you are serving vegetable dishes, try to choose a dish which complements your main course so that the flavours marry well and are neither too strong nor too bland.

1 Fennel with Cheese

Ingredients

3 fennel bulbs, quartered
Salt
50 g/2 oz Mozzarella cheese, cubed
50 g/2 oz/½ cup dried breadcrumbs
50 g/2 oz Parmesan cheese, grated
Freshly ground black pepper
25 g/1 oz/2 tbsp butter

Method

1. Cook the fennel in boiling salted water for about 20 minutes until just tender. Drain well and transfer to a shallow ovenproof dish.

2. Sprinkle the Mozzarella cheese over the fennel.

3. Mix together the breadcrumbs and Parmesan cheese and sprinkle over the fennel. Season to taste with salt and pepper and dot with butter.

4. Bake in a preheated oven at 200°C/400°F/gas mark 6 for about 10 minutes until crisp and golden brown. Serve immediately.

Serves 4

2 | Spicy Cauliflower

Ingredients

1 cauliflower, cut into florets
Salt
90 ml/6 tbsp olive oil
1 clove garlic, crushed
1 dried red chilli
Salt and freshly ground black pepper
15 ml/1 tbsp chopped fresh parsley

Method

1. Cook the cauliflower in boiling salted water for about 10 minutes until just tender but still slightly crisp.

2. Meanwhile, heat the oil in a heavy-based saucepan and fry the garlic and chilli over a very low heat for about 8 minutes. Remove and discard the garlic and chilli.

3. Drain the cauliflower and transfer to a warmed serving dish. Pour over the seasoned olive oil, sprinkle with salt, pepper and parsley and serve immediately.

Serves 4 to 6

3 Cauliflower with Olives

Ingredients

1 small cauliflower, cut into florets
Salt
10 green olives, stoned and chopped
1 onion, finely chopped
1 stick celery, finely chopped
30 ml/2 tbsp lemon juice
30 ml/2 tbsp chopped fresh parsley
15 ml/1 tbsp capers, chopped
90 ml/6 tbsp olive oil

Method

1. Cook the cauliflower in boiling salted water for about 10 minutes until just tender but still slightly crisp. Drain and rinse in cold water.

2. Mix the cauliflower with the olives, onion and celery.

3. Mix together the lemon juice, parsley and capers. Gradually whisk in the oil until the mixture is thoroughly blended. Pour over the vegetables and toss together gently.

4. Refrigerate for at least 1 hour before serving.

Serves 4

4 Stuffed Tomatoes

Ingredients

4 large ripe tomatoes
Salt
75 g/3 oz/⅓ cup long-grain rice
100 g/4 oz spinach
30 ml/2 tbsp olive oil
15 ml/1 tbsp pine kernels
1 clove garlic, crushed
15 ml/1 tbsp chopped fresh basil
Freshly ground black pepper
50 g/2 oz Parmesan cheese, grated
25 g/1 oz/2 tbsp butter

Method

1. Cut a slice off the top of each tomato and discard. Cut out the core of the tomatoes, scoop and discard the seeds. Sprinkle the insides with salt and stand the tomatoes upside down to drain.

2. Cook the rice in boiling salted water for about 10 minutes until tender. Drain.

3. Rinse the spinach and place it in a saucepan over a medium heat. Cover and steam for about 5 minutes until tender. Drain and gently squeeze out excess moisture.

4. Heat 15 ml/1 tbsp of oil in a heavy-based frying pan and fry the pine kernels quickly until lightly browned. Remove them from the pan and drain on kitchen paper.

5. Purée the pine kernels and spinach until coarsely chopped.

6.   Mix together the spinach mixture, the rice, garlic and basil and season to taste with salt and pepper. Stir in the cheese.

7.   Spoon the rice mixture into the tomatoes, dot the tops with butter and drizzle with the remaining oil and place in a greased shallow ovenproof dish. Bake in a preheated oven at 180°C/350°F/gas mark 4 for about 15 minutes until tender but not soft. Serve immediately.

Serves 4

5 | Aubergine and Mozzarella Fries

Ingredients

1 aubergine, sliced
Salt
5 ml/1 tsp dry yeast
375 ml/13 fl oz/1 ½ cups warm water
225 g/8 oz/2 cups plain flour
Freshly ground black pepper
75 ml/5 tbsp olive oil
175 g/6 oz Mozzarella cheese, sliced
10 ml/2 tsp chopped fresh basil
Oil for deep-frying
1 egg white
1 lemon, sliced

Method

1. Place the aubergine in a colander and sprinkle generously with salt. Cover with a plate and leave for about 30 minutes to drain off the bitter juices. Rinse and pat dry.

2. Mix the yeast with the warm water until dissolved. Beat in the flour and season with salt and pepper. Leave at room temperature for 30 minutes.

3. Heat the oil in a heavy-based frying pan and fry the aubergine slices, in batches if necessary, for about 5 minutes until golden brown on both sides. Remove from the pan and drain on kitchen paper.

4. Lay a slice of Mozzarella cheese on half the aubergine slices, sprinkle with basil and cover with another slice of aubergine to make a sandwich.

5. Heat the oil for deep-frying.

6. Whisk the egg white until stiff and fold it into the batter. Dip the aubergine sandwiches into the batter and fry in the oil for about 4 minutes, a few at a time, until lightly browned. Drain on kitchen paper, garnish with lemon slices and serve hot.

Serves 4 to 6

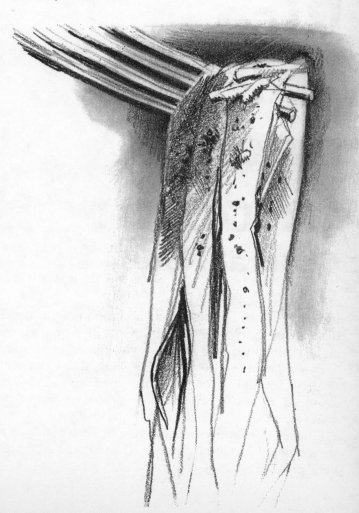

Rice, Polenta and Gnocchi

General Notes

Rice dishes can be the perfect accompaniment to rich Italian dishes, but are most often served as a dish on their own: delicious risottos made with meat, vegetables or seafoods.

Polenta is maize flour which is cooked like semolina. It can be served straight from the pan, topped with a rich meat sauce, or sliced or cubed and fried or grilled on its own or with cheeses.

Gnocchi are little balls usually made with potato or semolina then quickly and lightly boiled. Those made with spinach are very popular.

1 Rice with Peas

Ingredients

60 ml/4 tbsp olive oil
1 onion, chopped
1 stick celery, chopped
225 g/8 oz/1 cup arborio rice
120 ml/4 fl oz/½ cup dry white wine
375 ml/13 fl oz/1 ½ cups chicken stock
225 g/8 oz frozen peas
Salt and freshly ground black pepper

Method

1. Heat the oil in a heavy-based saucepan and fry the onion and celery for about 5 minutes until soft.

2. Add the rice and stir well until it is coated in the oil.

3. Add the wine and boil for 2 minutes, then gradually add the stock, a large spoonful at a time, waiting until the stock is absorbed before adding any more. The rice will take about 20 minutes to cook.

4. When you have added half the stock, stir in the peas and season to taste with salt and pepper. Continue to cook until the rice is tender and most of the liquid has been absorbed.

5. As a variation, you can add a little more stock and serve the dish in bowls to be eaten with spoons.

Serves 4

2 Rice Balls

Ingredients

15 ml/1 tbsp olive oil
15 ml/1 tbsp butter
1 small onion, finely chopped
100 g/4 oz/½ cup arborio rice
45 ml/3 tbsp dry white wine
250 ml/8 fl oz/1 cup chicken stock
Salt and freshly ground black pepper
45 ml/3 tbsp Parmesan cheese, grated
75 g/3 oz Mozzarella cheese, cubed
1 egg, beaten
50 g/2 oz/½ cup dry breadcrumbs
Oil for deep-frying

Method

1. Heat the oil and butter in a heavy-based saucepan and fry the onion for about 5 minutes until soft.

2. Add the rice and stir until it is well coated in the oil.

3. Add the wine and boil for 1 minute, then gradually add the stock, a large spoonful at a time, waiting until the stock is absorbed before adding any more. Season to taste with salt and pepper.

4. When all the stock has been absorbed and the rice is tender, stir in the Parmesan cheese and remove from the heat. Leave to cool.

5. Mould spoonfuls of the rice into balls around a cube of Mozzarella cheese. Roll them in egg, then breadcrumbs and fry them a few at a time in hot oil for about 5 minutes until crispy. Drain well on kitchen paper and serve hot.

Serves 4

3 Risotto Milanese

Ingredients

60 ml/4 tbsp butter
1 onion, finely chopped
225 g/8 oz/1 cup arborio rice
120 ml/4 fl oz/½ cup dry white wine
600 ml/1 pt/2 ½ cups chicken stock
Salt and freshly ground black pepper
A few saffron strands, crushed
60 ml/4 tbsp Parmesan cheese, grated

Method

1. Heat 45 ml/3 tbsp of butter in a heavy-based saucepan and fry the onion for about 5 minutes until soft.

2. Add the rice and stir until it is well coated in oil.

3. Add the wine and boil for 2 minutes, then gradually add the stock, a large spoonful at a time, waiting until the stock is absorbed before adding any more. The rice will take about 20 minutes to cook.

4. Season to taste with salt and pepper. Dissolve the saffron in a little boiling water and stir it into the risotto.

5. Stir in the remaining butter and the cheese and serve immediately.

Serves 4

Pepper Risotto

Ingredients

30 ml/2 tbsp olive oil
30 ml/2 tbsp butter
2 onions, chopped
1 clove garlic, crushed
1 small red pepper, seeded and diced
1 small green pepper, seeded and diced
1 small yellow pepper, seeded and diced
225 g/8 oz/1 cup arborio rice
450 ml/¾ pt/2 cups chicken or vegetable stock
1 courgette, diced
100 g/4 oz mushrooms, sliced
Salt and freshly ground black pepper
50 g/2 oz Parmesan cheese, grated

Method

1. Heat the oil and butter in a heavy-based saucepan and fry the onions and garlic for about 5 minutes until soft.

2. Add the peppers and fry gently for another 5 minutes.

3. Add the rice and stir until it is well covered in the oil.

4. Gradually add the stock, a large spoonful at a time, and cook until it is all absorbed before adding any more.

5. After about 10 minutes, add the courgette and mushrooms and season to taste with salt and pepper. Continue to add the stock and cook for a further 10 minutes until the rice is tender. Serve sprinkled with cheese.

Serves 4

5 Fried Polenta

Ingredients

750 ml/1¼ pts/3 cups water
A pinch of salt
175 g/6 oz/1 cup polenta
60 ml/4 tbsp sunflower oil

Method

1. Bring the water and salt to the boil in a heavy-based saucepan.

2. Gradually pour in the polenta, stirring all the time so that no lumps form. Simmer gently for about 40 minutes, stirring frequently, until the polenta is very thick and a spoon will stand upright in the centre.

3. The polenta can be served immediately with a meat dish.

4. For fried polenta, turn the polenta on to a plate or baking tin and leave to cool completely.

5. Unmould the polenta and cut it into 8 cm/3 in squares. Heat the oil in a heavy-based pan and fry the polenta over a medium heat for about 5 minutes until golden brown on all sides.

Serves 4

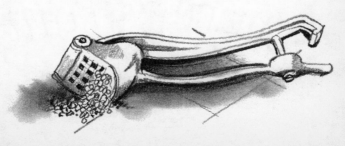

6 Grilled Polenta with Cheese

Ingredients

1 quantity Polenta (page 103)
100 g/4 oz Mozzarella cheese, sliced
15 ml/1 tbsp chopped fresh basil
Salt and freshly ground black pepper

Method

1. Make the polenta and leave it to cool.

2. Slice the polenta into thick slices and grill them on both sides until lightly browned.

3. Top each slice with a slice of cheese. Sprinkle with the basil and season to taste with salt and pepper. Return to the grill for about 4 minutes until the cheese is bubbling and beginning to turn brown.

Serves 4

7 Spinach Gnocchi

Ingredients

225 g/8 oz Ricotta cheese
450 g/1 lb cooked spinach, drained and chopped
50 g/2 oz Parmesan cheese, grated
100 g/4 oz/1 cup plain flour
2 eggs, beaten
A pinch of freshly grated nutmeg
Salt and freshly ground black pepper
50 g/2 oz butter, melted

Method

1. Rub the Ricotta cheese through a sieve and mix in the spinach, 15 ml/1 tbsp of Parmesan cheese and 45 ml/3 tbsp of flour. Mix in enough egg to make a smooth but firm mixture and season to taste with nutmeg, salt and pepper.

2. Stir everything together thoroughly, cover and refrigerate for 1 hour.

3. Sprinkle the work surface with flour and flour your hands. Take spoonfuls of the mixture and press them into small oval shapes. Dust them lightly but thoroughly in flour.

4. Bring a saucepan of salted water to the boil and cook the gnocchi a few at a time for about 5 minutes until slightly puffed and firm. The gnocchi will rise to the top of the water when cooked.

5. Arrange the cooked gnocchi in a shallow flameproof dish and pour over the melted butter. Sprinkle with the remaining cheese and grill for about 5 minutes until lightly browned.

Serves 4 to 6

8 Semolina Gnocchi

Ingredients

375 ml/13 fl oz/1 ½ cups water
375 ml/13 fl oz/1 ½ cups milk
A pinch of freshly grated nutmeg
Salt and freshly ground black pepper
175 g/6 oz/1 cup semolina
1 egg, beaten
50 g/2 oz Parmesan cheese, grated
75 g/3 oz/6 tbsp butter, melted

Method

1. Bring the water and milk to the boil in a heavy-based saucepan with the nutmeg, salt and pepper.

2. Gradually stir in the semolina, stirring briskly to avoid any lumps. Continue to cook, stirring frequently for about 15 minutes until the semolina is very thick.

3. Stir in the egg, 30 ml/2 tbsp of cheese and 15 ml/1 tbsp of butter. Turn into a well greased shallow baking tin and press down so that the mixture is about 1 cm/½ in thick. Refrigerate for 1 hour.

4. Cut 5 cm/2 in circles out of the semolina and lay them in overlapping rows in a shallow ovenproof dish. Pour over the remaining butter and sprinkle with the remaining cheese.

5. Bake in a preheated oven at 200°C/400°F/gas mark 6 for about 30 minutes until golden brown.

Serves 4 to 6

Pizzas
General Notes

There are as many varieties of pizza as there are people who make them. Making your own pizza dough is easy especially if you use a processor to take over the work of kneading and gives the best results. But if you are in a rush, try some of the very good ready-made pizza bases which you can buy in most supermarkets.

Once you have the basic principles, you can experiment with your own toppings to your heart's content.

Pizza Dough

Ingredients

300 ml/½ pt/1 ¼ cups warm water
5 ml/1 tsp sugar
15 g/½ oz/2 tsp dried yeast
450 g/1 lb/4 cups strong plain flour
5 ml/1 tsp salt

Method

1. To obtain the right temperature for the water, pour half the quantity of boiling water into a measuring jug, then top up with cold water. Pour the water into 2 jugs and sprinkle the sugar and yeast into 1 jug. Leave in a warm place for about 10 minutes until frothy.

2. Sift together the flour and salt. Gradually work in the yeast mixture and the remaining water, either by hand or in a food processor, until you have a smooth dough. Continue to knead until the dough is elastic and no longer sticky.

3. Place the dough in a bowl, cover with oiled clingfilm and leave in a warm place for about 2 hours until doubled in size.

4. Knead lightly again and use as directed in the recipe. This quantity of dough will make 1 x 30 cm/12 in pizza or 4 individual pizzas.

Serves 4

Garlic and Onion Pizza

Ingredients

1 quantity Pizza Dough (page 108)
150 ml/¼ pt/¾ cup olive oil
4 large onions, sliced
4 cloves garlic, chopped
Salt and freshly ground black pepper

Method

1. Make the dough and leave it to rise.

2. Work 15 ml/1 tbsp of olive oil into the dough then roll and press it out into a 30 cm/12 in circle and place in a greased pizza pan or on a greased baking sheet. Cover and leave to rest for 15 minutes.

3. Brush the dough generously with olive oil.

4. Spread with the onions, as many as you like, leaving a space around the edge of the pizza. Sprinkle with the garlic, as much as you dare, and season to taste with salt and pepper.

5. Bake in a preheated oven at 220°C/425°F/gas mark 7 for about 20 minutes until cooked through and beginning to brown on top. Serve immediately.

Serves 4

3 | Pepper and Mushroom Pizza

Ingredients

1 quantity Pizza Dough (page 108)
30 ml/2 tbsp olive oil
1 onion, chopped
1 clove garlic, crushed
400 g/14 oz canned tomatoes, chopped
45 ml/3 tbsp tomato purée
5 ml/1 tsp dried oregano
5 ml/1 tsp dried basil
Salt and freshly ground black pepper
1 red pepper, seeded and sliced
1 green pepper, seeded and sliced
100 g/4 oz mushrooms, sliced
100 g/4 oz Mozzarella cheese, shredded
100 g/4 oz Parmesan cheese, grated

Method

1. Make the dough and leave it to rise.

2. Work 15 ml/1 tbsp of olive oil into the dough then roll and press it out into a 30 cm/12 in circle and place in a greased pizza pan or on a greased baking sheet. Cover and leave to rest for 15 minutes.

3. Heat the remaining oil in a heavy-based pan and fry the onion and garlic for about 5 minutes until soft.

4. Add the tomatoes, tomato purée, oregano and basil and season to taste with salt and pepper. Cover and simmer gently for about 15 minutes.

5. Spread the sauce over the pizza dough and arrange the peppers and mushrooms on top. Sprinkle with the cheeses and season to taste with salt and pepper.

6. Bake in a preheated oven at 220°C/425°F/gas mark 7 for about 20 minutes until cooked through and golden brown.

Serves 4

Olive and Anchovy Pizza

Ingredients

1 quantity Pizza Dough (page 108)
30 ml/2 tbsp olive oil
1 onion, chopped
1 clove garlic, crushed
400 g/14 oz passata
50 g/2 oz green olives, stoned
50 g/2 oz black olives, stoned
50 g/2 oz anchovy fillets, drained
50 g/2 oz Parmesan cheese, grated
Salt and freshly ground black pepper

Method

1. Make the dough and leave it to rise.

2. Work 15 ml/1 tbsp of olive oil into the dough then roll and press it out into a 30 cm/12 in circle and place in a greased pizza pan or on a greased baking sheet. Cover and leave to rest for 15 minutes.

3. Heat the remaining oil in a heavy-based pan and fry the onion and garlic for about 5 minutes until soft.

4. Add the passata and simmer for 10 minutes.

5. Spread the tomato sauce over the pizza and arrange the olives and anchovies on top. Sprinkle with cheese and season to taste with salt and pepper.

6. Bake in a preheated oven at 220°C/425°F/gas mark 7 for about 20 minutes until cooked through.

Serves 4

5 | Calzone

Ingredients

1 quantity Pizza Dough (page 108)
30 ml/2 tbsp olive oil
1 onion, chopped
200 g/7 oz canned tomatoes, drained and chopped
100 g/4 oz cooked chicken, chopped
5 ml/1 tsp dried oregano
5 ml/1 tsp dried thyme
Salt and freshly ground black pepper

Method

1. Make the dough and leave it to rise.

2. Roll and press out the dough into a 30 cm/12 in circle and place in a greased pizza pan or on a greased baking sheet. Cover and leave to rest for 15 minutes.

3. Heat 15 ml/1 tbsp of oil in a heavy-based pan and fry the onion for about 5 minutes until soft. Add the tomatoes, chicken, oregano and thyme and season to taste with salt and pepper. Cover and simmer for 10 minutes.

4. Spread the tomato mixture over half the dough, brush the edges with water and fold over the other half of the dough. Press the edges together to seal. Brush with the remaining oil.

5. Bake in a preheated oven at 200°C/400°F/gas mark 6 for about 20 minutes until golden brown.

Serves 4

Spinach and Salami Pizza

Ingredients

1 quantity Pizza Dough (page 108)
30 ml/2 tbsp olive oil
1 onion, finely chopped
1 clove garlic, crushed
100 g/4 oz streaky bacon, chopped
175 g/6 oz cooked spinach
15 ml/1 tbsp chopped fresh basil
2 tomatoes, sliced
100 g/4 oz salami, sliced
100 g/4 oz Mozzarella cheese, cubed
Salt and freshly ground black pepper

Method

1. Make the dough and leave it to rise.

2. Work 15 ml/1 tbsp of olive oil into the dough then roll and press it out into a 30 cm/12 in circle and place in a greased pizza pan or on a greased baking sheet. Cover and leave to rest for 15 minutes.

3. Heat the remaining oil in a heavy-based pan and fry the onion, garlic and bacon for about 5 minutes until soft.

4. Add the spinach and basil and cook for a few minutes, stirring to combine the ingredients well.

5. Spread the spinach mixture over the dough. Arrange the tomatoes on top, then the salami, and top with the cheese. Season to taste with salt and pepper.

6. Bake in a preheated oven at 220°C/425°F/gas mark 7 for about 20 minutes until cooked through and golden brown.

Serves 4

7 Four-Cheese Pizza

Ingredients

1 quantity Pizza Dough (page 108)
60 ml/4 tbsp passata
4 large tomatoes, sliced
100 g/4 oz cooked ham, shredded
100 g/4 oz mushrooms, sliced
50 g/2 oz Mozzarella cheese, cubed
50 g/2 oz Gorgonzola cheese, grated
50 g/2 oz Parmesan cheese, grated
50 g/2 oz Pecorino cheese, grated
10 ml/2 tsp dried oregano
Salt and freshly ground black pepper

Method

1. Make the dough and leave it to rise.

2. Roll and press out the dough into a 30 cm/12 in circle and place in a greased pizza pan or on a greased baking sheet. Cover and leave to rest for 15 minutes.

3. Spread the dough with the passata. Arrange the tomatoes over the dough and sprinkle with the ham and mushrooms.

4. Sprinkle the cheeses in four quarters over the dough, sprinkle with the oregano and season to taste with salt and pepper.

5. Bake in a preheated oven at 220°C/425°F/gas mark 7 for about 20 minutes until cooked through and golden brown.

Serves 4

Salads

*Simple salads suitable for an
Italian meal can be made with
any fresh salad ingredients:
tomatoes, onions, fennel, lettuce.
Olives are a popular ingredient in
salads, and the dressings are
usually based on
olive oil.*

Tomato and Parmesan Salad

Ingredients

4 large tomatoes, sliced
100 g/4 oz Parmesan cheese, sliced
30 ml/2 tbsp olive oil
30 ml/2 tbsp chopped fresh parsley
Salt and freshly ground black pepper

Method

1. Arrange the tomatoes in a layer on a platter and top with a layer of cheese.

2. Sprinkle with olive oil, then with parsley and season to taste with salt and pepper.

Serves 4

2 Tomato and Salami Salad

Ingredients

100 g/4 oz salami, thinly sliced
90 ml/6 tbsp olive oil
Grated rind and juice of ½ lemon
1 clove garlic, crushed
30 ml/2 tbsp chopped fresh parsley
15 ml/1 tbsp chopped fresh basil
Salt and freshly ground black pepper
4 tomatoes, sliced

Method

1. Lay the salami in a shallow dish.

2. Mix together the olive oil, lemon rind and juice, garlic, half the parsley and the basil and season to taste with salt and pepper.

3. Pour the dressing over the salami and leave to stand for at least 1½ hours.

4. Lay a slice of salami on top of each slice of tomato and arrange on a serving dish. Pour any remaining dressing over the salad and serve sprinkled with the remaining parsley.

Serves 4

3 Fennel Salad

Ingredients

2 fennel bulbs, trimmed and thinly sliced
1 head radicchio, shredded
12 black olives, stoned
60 ml/4 tbsp olive oil
15 ml/1 tbsp lemon juice
10 ml/2 tsp anchovy paste
5 ml/1 tsp sugar
Salt and freshly ground black pepper

Method

1. Arrange the fennel, radicchio and olives in a salad bowl.

2. Mix together the oil, lemon juice, anchovy paste and sugar and season to taste with salt and pepper.

3. Pour the dressing over the salad, toss gently and serve immediately.

Serves 4

4 Avocado Salad

Ingredients

½ iceberg lettuce, shredded
1 avocado, peeled, stoned and sliced
15 ml/1 tbsp lemon juice
1 red pepper, seeded and sliced
2 tomatoes, sliced
½ cucumber, sliced
10 black olives, stoned
2 cloves garlic, crushed
10 ml/2 tsp chopped fresh basil
5 ml/1 tsp dried oregano
Salt and freshly ground black pepper
45 ml/3 tbsp olive oil
50 g/2 oz anchovy fillets, drained
15 ml/1 tbsp chopped fresh parsley

Method

1. Arrange the lettuce in the bottom of a salad bowl.

2. Toss the avocado in the lemon juice then mix in the pepper, tomatoes, cucumber, olives, and 1 clove of garlic. Sprinkle with the basil and oregano and season to taste with salt and pepper. Sprinkle over 15 ml/1 tbsp of olive oil and toss together. Spoon into the salad bowl, and garnish with a few of the anchovies. Cover and refrigerate for at least 1 hour.

3. Mix the remaining garlic, oil, anchovies with the parsley and mix together thoroughly, pressing with the back of a spoon until the anchovies disintegrate and you have a fairly smooth paste.

4. When ready to serve, spoon the anchovy mixture over the salad.

Serves 4

Tomato and Olive Salad

Ingredients

45 ml/3 tbsp white wine vinegar
15 ml/1 tbsp chopped fresh basil
5 ml/1 tsp sugar
Salt and freshly ground black pepper
90 ml/6 tbsp olive oil
3 tomatoes, cut into wedges
50 g/2 oz black olives, stoned
50 g/2 oz green olives, stoned
½ iceberg lettuce, shredded
½ head endive, shredded
A few radicchio leaves, shredded

Method

1. Mix together the wine vinegar, basil and sugar and season to taste with salt and pepper. Gradually whisk in the oil until the dressing is well blended.

2. Mix together the tomatoes and olives. Pour over the dressing, toss together carefully and leave to stand for about 40 minutes, tossing occasionally.

3. Arrange the lettuces in the bottom of a salad bowl and refrigerate until ready to serve.

4. Transfer the tomatoes and olives to the salad bowl and pour the remaining dressing over the salad.

Serves 4 to 6

Desserts

Typical Italian desserts include some delicious ice creams and sorbets which are wonderful for rounding off a rich meal. Naturally, we have included a recipe for the famous zabaglione, a delicious dessert of whisked egg yolks.

1 Cannoli

Ingredients

175 g/6 oz/1½ cups plain flour
30 ml/2 tbsp sugar
10 ml/2 tsp grated lemon rind
30 ml/2 tbsp butter, grated
1 egg
75 ml/5 tbsp marsala
750 g/1 ½ lb Ricotta cheese
250 g/9 oz icing sugar, sifted
5 ml/1 tsp ground cinnamon
45 ml/3 tbsp chopped mixed peel
Olive oil for deep-frying
50 g/2 oz chocolate, grated

Method

1. Mix together the flour, sugar and half the lemon rind and rub in the butter until the mixture resembles breadcrumbs.

2. Mix together the egg and marsala and stir into the flour until the mixture forms a dough. Cut the dough in half, wrap in clingfilm and refrigerate for 1 hour.

3. Beat the cheese until smooth. Reserve 30 ml/2 tbsp of icing sugar and beat the remainder into the cheese with the remaining lemon rind, cinnamon and mixed peel. Cover and refrigerate.

4. Roll out the dough pieces one at a time until very thin. Cut into rectangles 10 x 8 cm (4 x 3 in). Brush a short edge with water, fold the dough piece around an uncooked cannelloni pasta shell and seal the edges to form a tube.

5. Heat the oil in a heavy-based pan and fry the cannoli a few at a time for about 2 minutes until lightly browned. Drain on kitchen paper and remove the cannelloni.

6. When ready to serve, pipe the cheese filling into the pastry tubes, roll in icing sugar and dip the ends in chocolate. Serve immediately otherwise the pastry will go soggy.

Makes 16

2 Cassata

Ingredients

4 eggs, separated
225 g/8 oz/1⅓ cups icing sugar
500 ml/18 fl oz/2 cups whipping cream, beaten until firm
A few drops of almond essence
30 ml/2 tbsp cocoa powder
15 ml/1 tbsp cold water
50 g/2 oz milk chocolate
1 egg white
5 ml/1 tsp vanilla essence
90 ml/6 tbsp flaked almonds, toasted
12 glacé cherries, chopped
50 g/2 oz candied pineapple, chopped
3 dried apricots, chopped

Method

1. Place a 23 cm/9 in spring-form cake tin in the freezer.

2. Beat the egg whites until they form soft peaks then gradually beat in 175 g/6 oz/1 cup of icing sugar. Divide the mixture in half.

3. Lightly beat 2 egg yolks and fold them into half of the egg white mixture. Fold in one quarter of the cream and the almond essence. Pour the mixture into the chilled cake tin and freeze for at least 1 hour until firm.

4. Mix the cocoa and water until smooth.

5. Melt the chocolate over a bowl of simmering water and whisk in 2 egg yolks then the cocoa mixture.

6.   Fold one quarter of the cream into the remaining egg whites and sugar then fold in the chocolate mixture. Spread over the first layer in the cake tin and freeze for a further 1 hour until firm.

7.   Beat the remaining egg white until stiff then beat in the remaining sugar. Fold the egg whites into the remaining cream with the vanilla essence then fold in the fruit and nuts. Spread over the second layer and freeze for at least 6 hours until very firm.

8.   To serve, unmould the dessert and serve cut into wedges.

Serves 4

3 | Zabaglione

Ingredients

5 egg yolks
60 ml/4 tbsp caster sugar
120 ml/4 fl oz/½ cup marsala
60 ml/5 tbsp dry white wine
Langues de chat biscuits

Method

1. Place the egg yolks and sugar in the top of a double boiler and beat with a whisk until pale yellow and creamy.

2. Place the top of the boiler over simmering water over a low heat. Gradually beat in the marsala then the wine.

3. Keeping the heat very low, continue to beat the mixture, scraping the sides of the pan frequently, until the mixture is fluffy and thick enough to form soft mounds when dropped from the beaters. This will take about 20 minutes with a balloon whisk, or slightly less with a rotary or electric whisk.

4. Be careful not to let the water underneath boil as this will cause the custard to curdle. If the eggs do begin to curdle, remove them from the heat immediately and whisk quickly before returning to the heat.

5. When the zabaglione is ready, serve immediately with langues de chat biscuits.

Serves 4

Orange Granita

Ingredients

120 ml/4 fl oz/½ cup sweet white wine
120 ml/4 fl oz/½ cup water
100 g/4 oz/½ cup sugar
120 ml/4 fl oz/½ cup strained orange juice
1 egg white

Method

1. Mix the wine, water and sugar in a small saucepan and stir over a low heat until the sugar has dissolved. Cover the pan and boil for 1 minute. Uncover and simmer, without stirring, for 10 minutes. Remove from the heat, cool and refrigerate for about 30 minutes until the syrup is completely cool.

2. Stir the orange juice into the syrup and pour into a 23 cm/9 in round or square cake tin and freeze for 30 minutes.

3. Remove from the freezer and stir the mixture with a fork to break up the ice crystals. Freeze for 30 minutes. Chill a medium-sized mixing bowl.

4. Beat the egg white until stiff but not dry. Turn the orange syrup into the chilled bowl and beat with a fork or whisk until smooth.

5. Mix in the egg white and return the mixture to the cake tin. Spread evenly and freeze for 15 minutes.

6. Stir the mixture again, then cover with foil and freeze for at least 4 hours until firm.

Serves 4

5 Rum Custard Dessert

Ingredients

6 eggs
275 g/10 oz/1¼ cups sugar
Salt
150 g/5 oz/1¼ cups plain flour
75 ml/5 tbsp cornflour
750 ml/1¼ pts/3 cups milk
2 egg yolks
30 ml/2 tbsp butter
5 ml/1 tsp vanilla essence
225 g/8 oz strawberries
75 ml/5 tbsp rum
60 ml/4 tbsp icing sugar
600 ml/1 pt/2½ cups whipping cream

Method

1. Beat the eggs until foamy. Beat in 175 g/6 oz/¾ cup of sugar, a little at a time, and continue to beat for 3 minutes.

2. Gradually fold in the flour, a little at a time, with a pinch of salt.

3. Spoon the mixture into a greased and floured 25 cm/10 in spring-form cake tin and bake in a preheated oven at 180°C/350°F/gas mark 4 for about 40 minutes until golden brown and a skewer inserted into the centre comes out clean. Remove from the tin and leave to cool.

4. Mix the remaining sugar with a pinch of salt, the cornflour and milk in a heavy-based saucepan. Gradually bring to the boil, stirring continuously, then simmer for 3 minutes. Remove from the heat.

5.   Whisk the egg yolks in a bowl then gradually whisk in a little of the hot milk. Whisk the egg yolk mixture back into the milk in the saucepan and cook over a very low heat, stirring continuously, for 1 minute.

6.   Pour the custard into a bowl, stir in the butter and vanilla essence until the butter has melted then cover with greaseproof paper and leave to cool, stirring occasionally.

7.   Reserve a few strawberries for garnish and thinly slice the remainder.

8.   Assemble the cake in the cleaned cake tin. Slice the cake horizontally into three layers. Brush the top of each layer with rum. Spread half the custard over the bottom layer of cake and arrange half the strawberries on top. Place the second layer on top and spread with the remaining custard and strawberries. Top with the final layer of cake. Cover and refrigerate for 12 hours.

9.   When ready to serve, whisk the cream and icing sugar and spread most of it over the top and sides of the cake. Use a little to pipe decorations on the top and garnish with the reserved fruit just before serving.

Makes 1 x 25 cm/8 in cake

Biscuits and Cakes

Nuts, particularly almonds, feature heavily in Italian biscuits and cakes, giving a wonderful texture and interest to the finished results.

1 Amaretti

Ingredients

200 g/7 oz/1¾ cups ground almonds
225 g/8 oz/1 cup caster sugar
2 egg whites
2.5 ml/½ tsp vanilla essence
A few drops of almond essence
24 whole blanched almonds

Method

1. Mix together the ground almonds, sugar, egg whites, vanilla essence and almond essence.

2. Beat the mixture slowly until well combined, then beat quickly for about 5 minutes and leave to stand for 5 minutes. The mixture should be a thick batter.

3. Pipe the batter into small rounds on a greased baking sheet and press a whole almond into the top of each one. Bake in a preheated oven at 190°C/375°F/gas mark 5 for about 15 minutes until golden brown. Cool on wire racks and serve cold.

Makes about 24 biscuits

2 Orange Liqueur Creams

Ingredients

200 g/7 oz/1¾ cups plain flour
10 ml/2 tsp baking powder
5 ml/1 tsp salt
50 g/2 oz/¼ cup butter
100 g/4 oz/½ cup sugar
5 ml/1 tsp grated lemon rind
1 egg
60 ml/4 tbsp milk
5 ml/1 tsp vanilla essence
15 ml/1 tbsp orange liqueur
150 ml/¼ pt/⅔ cup whipping cream, whipped
30 ml/2 tbsp icing sugar

Method

1. Mix together the flour, baking powder and salt. Rub in the butter until the mixture resembles fine breadcrumbs. Stir in the sugar and lemon rind.

2. Mix together the egg, milk and vanilla essence. Stir this into the flour mixture and work together to a soft dough. Knead the dough until smooth then roll into a ball, cover and refrigerate for 1 hour.

3. Roll out the dough on a floured surface to 1 cm/½ in thick. Cut out 5 cm/2 in circles with a pastry cutter and arrange them on greased baking sheets. Reroll and cut the trimmings.

4. Bake in a preheated oven at 180°C/350°F/gas mark 4 for about 20 minutes until golden brown. Transfer to a wire rack to cool.

5.   Cut the biscuits in half horizontally and brush the cut sides with liqueur. Sandwich together with cream and dust with icing sugar.

Makes about 24 biscuits

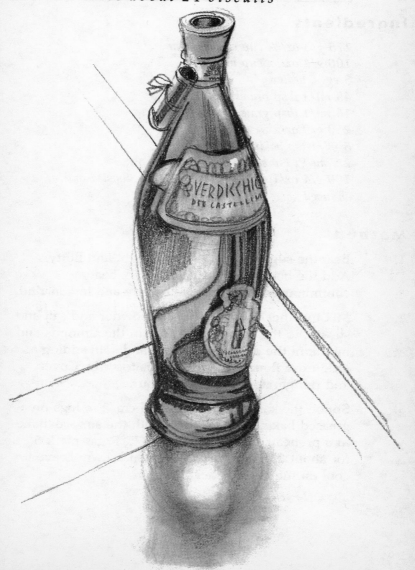

3 Brandy and Nut Biscuits

Ingredients

175 g/6 oz/¾ cup caster sugar
100 g/4 oz/½ cup butter
3 eggs, beaten
45 ml/3 tbsp brandy
15 ml/1 tbsp grated lemon rind
250 g/9 oz/2 ¼ cups plain flour
5 ml/1 tsp baking powder
2.5 ml/½ tsp salt
100 g/4 oz/1 cup blanched almonds, toasted and chopped

Method

1. Beat the sugar and butter until light and fluffy. Add the beaten eggs one at a time, beating continuously, then add the brandy and lemon rind.

2. Mix together the flour, baking powder and salt and stir it into the egg mixture. Stir in the almonds and mix until the dough is smooth and soft, adding a little extra flour if the mixture is too wet. Cover and refrigerate for at least 1 hour.

3. Spoon the soft dough into 2 x 5 cm/2 in logs on a greased baking sheet and smooth the surface. Bake in a preheated oven at 190°C/375°F/gas mark 5 for about 25 minutes until golden brown. Leave to cool on the baking sheet.

4. Cut the logs diagonally into 1.5 cm/½ in thick slices and lay them on ungreased baking sheets. Bake in a preheated oven at 180°C/350°F/gas mark 4 for about 10 minutes until the tops are lightly browned, then turn the biscuits and bake for a further 10 minutes. Cool on wire racks and store in an airtight container.

Makes about 48 biscuits

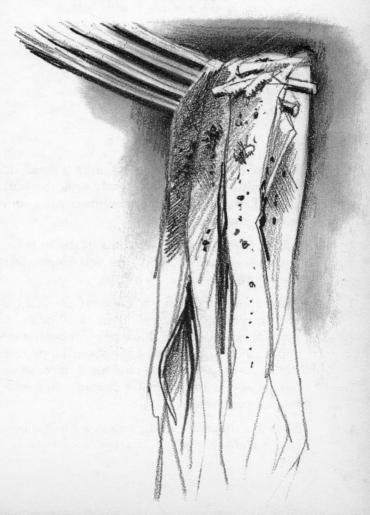

4 Florentine Biscuits

Ingredients

50 g/2 oz/¼ cup butter
50 g/2 oz/¼ cup sugar
15 ml/1 tbsp double cream
25 g/1 oz/¼ cup flaked almonds, chopped
25 g/1 oz/¼ cup walnuts, finely chopped
6 glacé cherries, chopped
15 ml/1 tbsp sultanas, chopped
15 ml/1 tbsp finely grated lemon rind
15 ml/1 tbsp chopped preserved ginger
45 ml/3 tbsp plain flour
100 g/4 oz chocolate

Method

1. Mix the butter, sugar and cream in a small heavy-based saucepan and heat gently until the butter melts. Bring to the boil and simmer for 1 minute, stirring continuously.

2. Remove from the heat and stir in the nuts, cherries, sultanas, lemon rind and ginger. Stir in the flour.

3. Place spoonfuls of the mixture on greased baking sheets, spacing them well apart to allow them to spread while cooking. Bake in a preheated oven at 180°C/350°F/gas mark 4 for about 10 minutes until browned. Leave to cool for 2 minutes on the baking sheets then transfer carefully to a wire rack to cool completely.

4. Melt the chocolate in the top of a double boiler over simmering water. Leave to cool slightly.

5. When the biscuits are cool, turn them upside down on a baking sheet lined with greaseproof paper. Spread the chocolate over the biscuits, leave it to cool very slightly, then mark a wavy pattern on the chocolate with a fork. Leave to cool completely.

Makes about 24 biscuits

5 Panettone Cake

Ingredients

50 g/2 oz/¼ cup sugar
30 ml/2 tbsp warm water
5 ml/1 tsp dried yeast
90 ml/6 tbsp milk
50 g/2 oz/¼ cup butter
2.5 ml/½ tsp salt
1 egg
2 egg yolks
275 g/10 oz/2 ½ cups plain flour
25 g/1 oz/2 tbsp chopped mixed peel
75 g/3 oz/½ cup sultanas
50 g/2 oz/⅓ cup pine kernels
10 ml/2 tsp grated lemon rind
30 ml/2 tbsp icing sugar

Method

1. Stir 5 ml/1 tsp of sugar into the warm water, sprinkle on the yeast and leave to stand in a warm place until frothy.

2. Heat the milk, butter, sugar and salt in a small saucepan until the butter has melted. Pour into a large bowl and leave to cool until lukewarm.

3. Whisk the egg and egg yolks into the milk. Stir in 100 g/4 oz/1 cup of flour and beat for 1 minute. Whisk in the yeast mixture and stir in 100 g/4 oz/ 1 cup of flour to form a soft dough. Knead for 3 minutes.

4. Stir in the mixed peel, sultanas, pine kernels and lemon rind and knead until the dough is elastic and no longer sticky. Cover with oiled clingfilm and leave in a warm place for about 1 hour until doubled in size.

5. Spread the remaining flour on a work surface and knead the dough until smooth and elastic, working in as much flour as necessary. Cover with oiled clingfilm and leave to rise again for about 1 hour until double in size.

6. Punch down the dough and knead it briefly. Shape into balls and place in a well-greased 900 g/2 lb loaf tin. Cover and leave to rise for 1 hour until doubled in size.

7. Brush the top with a little melted butter and cut a shallow cross in the top. Bake in a preheated oven at 200°C/400°F/gas mark 6 for 15 minutes then reduce the temperature to 160°C/325°F/gas mark 3 and bake for a further 50 minutes until golden brown. Leave to cool in the tin for 10 minutes before turning out on to a wire rack to cool completely. Dust with icing sugar before serving.

Makes 1 x 900g/2 lb cake

6 Siena Cake

Ingredients

100 g/4 oz/1 cup blanched almonds, toasted and
  chopped
100 g/4 oz/1 cup hazelnuts, toasted, skinned and
  chopped
50 g/2 oz/⅓ cup chopped dried apricots
25 g/1 oz/3 tbsp chopped mixed peel
75 g/3 oz/⅔ cup plain flour
30 ml/2 tbsp cocoa
5 ml/1 tsp ground cinnamon
2.5 ml/½ tsp freshly grated nutmeg
A pinch of ground coriander
120 ml/4 fl oz/½ cup honey
75 g/3 oz/⅓ cup sugar
50 g/2 oz chocolate, melted
30 ml/2 tbsp icing sugar

Method

1.   Mix together the nuts, apricots, mixed peel, flour,
     cocoa, cinnamon, nutmeg and coriander.

2.   Mix the honey and sugar in a small saucepan and
     heat gently until the sugar dissolves. Bring to the
     boil and simmer over a medium heat, without
     stirring, for about 5 minutes until a drop of the
     syrup forms a soft ball when dropped into cold
     water.

3.   Stir the syrup into the fruit and nut mixture, then
     stir in the melted chocolate.

4.   Spoon the mixture into a greased and line 20 cm/8
     in cake tin and level the top. Bake in a preheated
     oven at 160°C/325°F/gas mark 3 for about 35
     minutes.

5. Leave to cool for 5 minutes before removing from the tin and cooling completely on a wire rack. Keep for at least 1 day wrapped in kitchen foil before serving dusted with icing sugar and cut into very thin slices.

Makes 1 x 20 cm/8 in cake

7 Ricotta Cake

Ingredients

75 g/3 oz plain flour
30 ml/2 tbsp cocoa powder
75 g/3 oz butter
75 g/3 oz caster sugar
250 ml/8 fl oz/1 cup Ricotta cheese
150 g/5 oz/⅔ cup caster sugar
45 ml/3 tbsp orange liqueur
100 g/4 oz milk chocolate, grated
25 g/1 oz crystallised ginger, chopped
8 glacé cherries, chopped
150 ml/¼ pt/⅔ cup water
100 g/4 oz/½ cup butter
75 g/3 oz/½ cup blanched almonds, toasted

Method

1.   Beat together the flour, cocoa, butter and sugar until smooth. Pour the mixture into a greased 20 cm/8 in round cake tin and bake in a preheated oven for about 20 minutes until risen and firm. Remove from the oven and leave to cool.

2.   Rub the cheese through a sieve. Beat in 60 ml/4 tbsp of the sugar and half the liqueur then stir in one-quarter of the chocolate, the ginger and cherries.

3.   Mix together 30 ml/2 tbsp of sugar with the remaining liqueur and 75 ml/5 tbsp of water in a small saucepan. Cook, stirring, over a low heat until the sugar dissolves then bring to the boil and simmer for 1 minute. Remove from the heat and leave to cool.

4.   Cut the cake horizontally into 3 layers. Brush the top of each layer with the cooled syrup. Spread two layers with the ricotta mixture, pile them on top of each other and top with the remaining cake.

5.   Melt the remaining chocolate, stirring continuously, in the top of a double boiler over simmering water. Remove from the heat and leave to cool slightly.

6.   Meanwhile, heat the remaining water and sugar until the sugar dissolves then bring to the boil and remove from the heat. Leave to cool to room temperature.

7.   Beat the butter until smooth and creamy. Beat in the cooled syrup, then beat in the chocolate. Spread the icing on the top and sides of the cake and press the almonds into the icing. Cover and refrigerate for at least 4 hours before serving.

Serves 6 to 8

8 Almond Biscuits

Ingredients

225 g/8 oz/2 cups ground almonds
15 ml/1 tbsp plain flour
5 ml/1 tsp grated lemon rind
1 egg white
100 g/4 oz/½ cup caster sugar
30 ml/2 tbsp honey
A few drops of vanilla essence

Method

1. Mix together the almonds, flour and lemon rind.

2. Beat the egg white until stiff. Remove and reserve 5 ml/1 tsp. Beat 60 ml/4 tbsp of sugar into the egg white, then beat in the honey. Mix this into the almond mixture.

3. Make small sausage shapes of the mixture on a greased baking sheet and flatten the ends. Bake in a preheated oven at 150°C/300°F/gas mark 2 for about 20 minutes until lightly browned.

4. Meanwhile, beat the reserved egg white with the remaining sugar and the vanilla essence. Brush over the cooked biscuits and leave to cool and harden.

Makes about 16 biscuits

9 | Fruit and Nut Cake

Ingredients

3 eggs
100 g/4 oz/½ cup caster sugar
150 g/5 oz/1¼ cups chopped mixed nuts
100 g/4 oz/⅔ cup dried figs, chopped
75 g/3 oz/½ cup chopped mixed peel
75 g/3 oz milk chocolate, grated
150 g/5 oz/1½ cups plain flour
10 ml/2 tsp baking powder
5 ml/1 tsp salt

Method

1. Beat the eggs and sugar for about 5 minutes until pale yellow and thick.

2. Mix together the nuts, figs, mixed peel and chocolate and fold them into the eggs.

3. Sift the flour, baking powder and salt gradually into the mixture and fold together.

4. Spoon the mixture into a greased 900 g/2 lb loaf tin and bake in a preheated oven for about 1 hour until golden brown and firm.

5. Cool in the tin for 5 minutes before turning out on to a wire rack to finish cooling.

Makes 1 x 900 g/2 lb cake

Sauces

There are many simple Italian sauces that you can use with pasta or to serve as accompaniments to simple dishes.

1 Tomato Sauce

Ingredients

15 ml/1 tbsp olive oil
1 large onion, finely chopped
1 clove garlic, crushed
400 g/14 oz passata
45 ml/3 tbsp tomato purée
A pinch of dried thyme
A pinch of dried rosemary
Salt and freshly ground black pepper

Method

1. Heat the oil and fry the onion and garlic for about 5 minutes until the onion is soft but not browned.

2. Add the remaining ingredients and bring to the boil. Simmer over a low heat for about 10 minutes, stirring occasionally.

Serves 4

2 Tomato and Herb Sauce

Ingredients

30 ml/2 tbsp olive oil
15 ml/1 tbsp butter
750 g/1 ½ lb passata
15 ml/1 tbsp chopped fresh basil
30 ml/2 tbsp chopped fresh parsley
Salt and freshly ground black pepper

1. Heat the oil and butter and stir in the passata and basil. Bring to the boil then simmer for about 30 minutes until the sauce has thickened and reduced to about 600 ml/1 pt/2½ cups.

2. Stir in the parsley and season to taste with salt and pepper.

3. This sauce is delicious served with spaghetti.

Serves 4

3 Pizza Sauce

Ingredients

30 ml/2 tbsp olive oil
3 cloves garlic, crushed
750 g/1 ½ lb passata
5 ml/1 tsp dried oregano
Salt and freshly ground black pepper
30 ml/2 tbsp chopped fresh parsley

Method

1. Heat the oil and fry the garlic until golden.

2. Stir in the passata and oregano and season to taste with salt and pepper. Bring to the boil and simmer for about 30 minutes until the sauce is reduced to about 600 ml/1 pt/2 ½ cups.

3. Stir in the parsley and adjust the seasoning to taste.

4. This is delicious with spaghetti or used as a pizza topping.

Serves 4

Chianti Putto

White Sauce

Ingredients

45 ml/3 tbsp butter
45 ml/3 tbsp plain flour
200 ml/7 fl oz/scant 1 cup water
250 ml/8 fl oz/1 cup milk
Salt and freshly ground black pepper

Method

1. Melt the butter in a small saucepan. Stir in the flour and cook, stirring, for 1 minute.

2. Mix together the water and milk and gradually stir it into the flour. Bring to the boil and simmer over a low heat, stirring continuously, until the mixture thickens.

Serves 4

5 Anchovy Sauce

Ingredients

150 ml/¼ pt/⅔ cup olive oil
1 clove garlic, crushed
50 g/2 oz anchovy fillets, drained and chopped
Freshly ground black pepper

Method

1. Place the oil, garlic and anchovies in a heavy-based pan and heat over a gentle heat, crushing the anchovies until they form a smooth creamy sauce. Season to taste with pepper.

2. Serve hot over cauliflower or other vegetables; fish or pasta.

Makes about 150 ml/¼ pt/⅔ cup

6 Pesto Sauce

Ingredients

75 ml/5 tbsp olive oil
30 ml/2 tbsp pine kernels
1 clove garlic, crushed
1 large bunch fresh basil, chopped
Salt and freshly ground black pepper
75 g/3 oz Parmesan cheese, grated

Method

1. Heat half the oil in a heavy-based saucepan and fry the pine kernels for about 1 minute until lightly browned. Remove from the pan and drain on kitchen paper.

2. Purée the pine kernels with the garlic, basil and remaining oil until very finely chopped.

3. Stir in the cheese and season to taste with salt and pepper.

4. Store in the refrigerator for up to 1 week in an airtight jar, covered with a thin layer of olive oil, or freeze in small containers and thaw thoroughly before using.

Makes about 150 ml/¼ pt/⅔ cup

7 | Mayonnaise

Ingredients

1 egg
1 egg yolk
5 ml/1 tsp mustard powder
5 ml/1 tsp salt
30 ml/2 tbsp lemon juice
15 ml/1 tbsp white wine vinegar
375 ml/13 fl oz/1 ½ cups olive or sunflower oil
Freshly ground black pepper

Method

1. Place the egg, egg yolk, mustard, salt, lemon juice and wine vinegar in a blender and mix together.

2. Add 120 ml/4 fl oz/½ cup of oil and blend together.

3. With the blender running, very slowly pour in the remaining oil. You will hear the tone of the blender change as the mayonnaise thickens. Season to taste with pepper.

Makes about 450 ml/¾ pt/2 cups

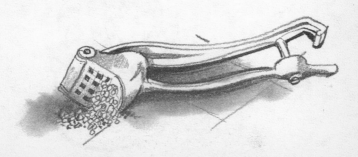

8 Tartare Sauce

Ingredients

1 quantity Mayonnaise (page 155)
1 spring onion, finely chopped
15 ml/1 tbsp capers, drained and chopped
1 sweet gherkin, chopped
30 ml/2 tbsp chopped fresh parsley

Method

1. Make the mayonnaise.

2. Stir in the remaining ingredients, turn into an airtight jar and refrigerate until required.

Makes about 450 ml/¾ pt/2 cups

Index